BUSINESS SURVIVAL WORKBOOK
CREATING SUSTAINABLE SUCCESS

Business Survival

Transform

Innovate

Stabilize

Grow

Building a Strategic Plan and Implementing It!

The Vision Tree, Ltd.

Joanne H. Osmond
Claudia J. Pannell

This publication is designed to provide accurate and authoritative information in regard to the subject-matter covered. It is sold with the understanding that the publisher is not engaged in rendering legal, accounting, or other professional services. If legal advice or other expert assistance is required, the services of a competent professional should be sought.

Editorial Assistant: Barbara L. Coffing
Cover Design: Joanne H. Osmond
Copyright © 2009 by The Vision Tree, Ltd.

Published by The Vision Tree, Ltd.
216 Waterbury Circle, Lake Villa, IL 60046
Jo@TheVisionTree.com
847.356.7550 Fax: 847.356.3783

Printed in the United States of America

ISBN: 978-1-933334-20-2

Acknowledgement

In the local community where I live and work, there are many Small Business Owners and Professionals who continue to amaze me with their hard work and their continuing support for others around them. Of special note are two women (Dr. Pamela Norley and Mary Erl) who are part of a small group which was formed in 2003 and six years later we continue to meet every month. Pam, Mary, Claudia Pannell, and Barbara Coffing continue to ground me in reality and offer a continuous flow of advice that builds me up and helps me continue to excel. To the many women business owners across the world, I say thank you for I know how much women can accomplish when they work together.

Table of Contents

Business Survival for Existing Businesses

With an intense schedule to meet and the time constraints of a business, Small Business Owners learn quickly how to prioritize their strengths and weaknesses. To sustain growth they learn how to quickly validate their strategic direction. They understand the importance of what can be delegated or outsourced and what should be maintained for strategic advantage. They identify and document important decisions for a strong structural foundation for their business's long-term survival. Small Business Owners become familiar with the resources available that can add to their own wealth of knowledge for their continued success. Concepts they address include:

- Strategic decision-making skills
- Sustainable competitive advantage
- Transforming entrepreneurial roles
- Building for growth and aligning operations
- Profitability for survival and beyond

Small Business Strategic Planning

Ask yourself key questions as you review your business plan. To take your business to the next level, follow the steps in a simple process to build a strategic implementation plan.

1. **Strategize** – Define who you are? What is important to you? What is your Focus? What is your SWOT (Strengths, Weaknesses, Opportunities, and Threats)?
2. **Plan** – How are you going to implement the strategy? Where are you going to assign your resources? Are your goals written down? Are your goals S.M.A.R.T.?
3. **Implement** – What are the initiatives that you execute to align your organization with the strategy you defined? How are you making it happen? How are you aligning your resources to the plan and strategy?
4. **Reflect** – What was the impact on the organization? What needs to be changed? What challenges might you face when you implement your plan?

Repeat the same steps each time you focus on a new business strategy. As you build your plan include strategies that focus on transforming, stabilizing, growing, and innovating your business.

Business Survival Workbook – Creating Sustainable Success includes the following deliverables designed to ensure sustainable growth.

- **Networking Survival Kit**

  Four Networking Tactics will assist the participants in developing networking survival skills

- **One-Page Strategic Plan (1-PSP™)**

  A Strategic Plan designed for a small business to take their business to the next level

- **Seven–Touch Marketing Plan (7-TMP™)**

  A simple Marketing Plan to ensure advertizing that will reach all of the desired customers

- **One-Page Strategic Indicators (1-PSI™)**

  A Dashboard to monitor the progress of the 1-PSP (Strategic Plan)

Pay attention to what matters most and transform, stabilize, grow, and innovate your business to achieve sustainable success using the simple planning cycle to **SPIR** (Strategize, Plan, Implement, and Reflect) to success.

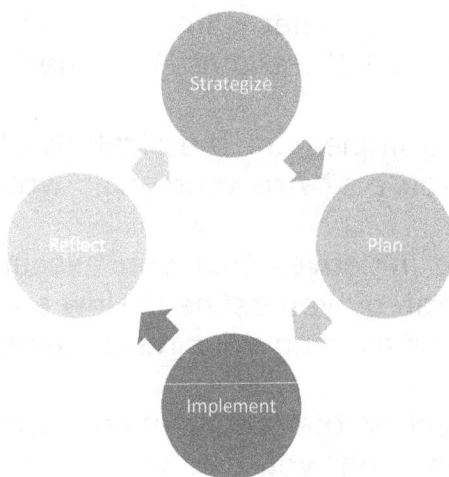

~ Networking ~

Network Survival Kit

The objective of the Network Survival Kit is to expose us to techniques for networking that may not be intuitive or taught in other settings. Networking is a learned skill that is vital to business survival. It is a powerful tool that will increase a business owner's visibility and develop relationships with key contacts. Over the next four weeks, four networking techniques will be experienced. The basic premise of these techniques is: To be successful at networking, we will share information with others and learn how to connect with others to determine not what others can do for us but what they can do to help others.

When we enter a room, we will look for ways to make a difference and be of service to others. Every person has valuable information to share and by seeking to help others, we will be helped in return. The energy of giving provides a powerful motive to listen carefully to people, waiting for a chance to give assistance. This other-focused giving attitude changes the dynamics of meeting new people and makes us positive, enthusiastic, and genuinely curious about others.

Networking is really about giving instead of getting and when that is achieved, there is a new level of success. By adopting this powerful attitude, we will immediately be eager to meet new people because they know they can make a positive difference in our lives. Many of the ideas in these exercises are found in "Growing Your Business Through Principled Networking" by Julia Hubbel and published by Ernst & Young LLP.

> **Week One** – By asking probing questions, discover something wonderful about someone in the class. Be prepared to introduce your partner and share what is wonderful about the other person.
>
> **Week Two** – Relate to others who are different from you and come to a common agreement using the 4 Steps to Connecting.
>
> **Week Three** – Look for opportunities to help others. Ask, "What can I do for you?" then listen with the intent to serve.
>
> **Week Four** – List who you know and share your resources, (i.e., accountants, attorneys, bankers, landscapers). The more you give, the more you will receive.

"Networking is one of three key areas that small businesses should focus on, along with employing technology and developing strategic alliances. Networking is actively making professional relationships, developing and maintaining those relationships, and leveraging them for the benefit of all parties."

Jim Blasingame

'The longest journey begins with the first step.' Chinese Proverb

It is time to step forward and take networking to the next level.

Week One

Assignment: By asking probing questions, discover something wonderful about someone in the class. Be prepared to introduce your partner and share what is wonderful about the other person.

Put your attention on the other person, not you! When your focus is on asking the other person about his or her background and opinions, you're making it easy for them to talk. Relax and enjoy the conversation because you don't have to be clever or entertaining. Listen to understand: Pay close attention and listen for intriguing information. Whether approaching a group or one person, come armed with good questions.

Ask open-end questions and statements which begin in: Who, What, When, Where, Why, and How. Ask for more information or details. Act like a reporter and interview your partner so they will tell you the whole story. You'll never find yourself without a conversational partner and your popularity will soar, simply because you aren't the one who has to be witty and interesting. Let others shine and as you do, you'll be making friends.

No matter whom you're talking to, there is something interesting, even wonderful about that person. Make it a point to find out what that is. Put aside your first impressions. When you can do this, the person's real value can come through. Ask lots of probing questions. If you try hard enough, you will stumble on a truly-interesting story. People are full of surprises. When you focus on what other people have to offer, many opportunities open up for you both.

Ask questions like:

- Tell me about your work. What made you choose it?
- Tell me more about your clients.
- Who do you prefer to work with?
- Why did you choose to live here?
- What's your favorite customer story?

Or ask more personal questions like:

- What was the biggest challenge you've overcome?
- What is the biggest problem you're trying to solve right now?
- What's the funniest thing that has happened to you in your work?

If you don't feel as though you have anything interesting to say about yourself, you're pretty normal. Imagine what happens when you put your attention to finding something interesting about your conversational partner, who often has the same beliefs about himself. When you discover something wonderful, you discover it together.

Which questions were the easiest for you to use in a conversation? List additional questions you asked that helped you determine something wonderful about your partner.

Week Two

Assignment: Relate to others who are different from you and come to a common agreement using the **4 Steps to Connecting**.

"Two people see the same object, but they never see it in such a way that the images they receive are absolutely identical." *Psychological Types* by CG Jung. People do not approach networking the same way. There are basically four groups of people, plus some people feel one way sometimes and another way at other times.

- **You love group functions.** You walk in and notice who is new. You walk up to them and introduce yourself. You explain who you are and what you do so the new person will feel comfortable.

- **You prefer small familiar groups.** You walk in and walk directly to someone you know. If a stranger asks a question, you will only provide a short response until you get to know them better.

- **You prefer business functions.** You walk in with a list. (It may be in your head or written down.) You walk directly to the first person on your list and complete the task before going to the next person on your list.

- **You prefer a lecture or meeting where you learn something new.** You listen carefully to discussions, and then ask detail questions about any subject that interests you.

While it is easy to identify people who are like you, you may not know how to recognize other types. It is important to adapt and connect to others.

Do's and Don'ts for Observers	Do's and Don'ts for Directors
Do	**Do**
Be well prepared and thorough	Be direct and to the point
Put things in writing	Focus on results and objectives
Let me consider all the details	Be brief, be bright, and be gone
Don't	**Don't**
Get too close or hug me	Hesitate or dilly-dally
Be flippant on important issues	Focus on feelings
Change my routine without notice	Try to take over
Do's and Don'ts for Supporters	**Do's and Don'ts for Inspirers**
Do	**Do**
Be patient and supportive	Be friendly and sociable
Slow down and work at my pace	Be entertaining and stimulating
Ask my opinion and give me time to answer	Be open and flexible
Don't	**Don't**
Take advantage of my good nature	Bore me with details
Push me to make quick decisions	Tie me down with routine
Spring last-minute surprises	Ask me to work alone

Develop Usable Networking Strategies - 4 Steps to Connecting

1st Step to Simply Connect
- Engage empathically and establish a "win-win" partnership.
- Before jumping straight to the "task" enter the conversation in the spirit of partnership.
- Show empathy towards them and establish rapport.

2nd Step to Simply Connect
- Understand the other person by listening empathically first.
- The second stage is to connect and listen.
- Seek to understand the other person's point of view.

3rd Step to Simply Connect
- Be understood by the other person by clearly communicating your point of view.
- After you have heard the other person and when the other person feels heard, then clearly communicate your point of view.
- Don't start with Step 3. Complete Step 1 and Step 2 before Step 3.

4th Step to Simply Connect
- Discuss the issues logically and rationally to reach agreement.
- Now a "space" has been created for a logical discussion to find a "win-win" solution.
- The "space" created will also enable more creative solutions to be found.
- There may be greater understanding of each other's perspectives.

Advice for successful networking:
Directors
- Occasionally ask the listeners if they are following you.
- Put yourself in the other person's shoes.
- Consider the feelings of the receiver.

Inspirers
- Ensure the receiver has a chance to comment or ask you questions.
- Do not ignore signs of confusion from the receiver.

Supporters
- Be sure your words match your tone and body.
- Look at the receiver. Make eye contact.

Observers
- Be clear about what you say.
- Don't be vague; on the other hand, don't complicate what you say with too much detail.
- Vary your tone and your pace.

You connect with people on a daily basis - family members, neighbors, co-workers, team members, etc. You will improve your relationships if you pause and think about the affect you have on each other.

Week Three

Assignment: Look for opportunities to help others. Ask, "What can I do for you?" then listen with the intent to serve.

This attitude takes networking to another level. Look for an opportunity to make a difference in another person's life, whether it's a recommendation for a good restaurant, a referral to your network of friends, a suggestion or an idea, a job opportunity you know about or an introduction to a friend. Be on the lookout for anything you can offer. Dr. Wayne Dyer says in *You'll See It When You Believe It*, "in a network the purpose is to give power away." In other words, the more you give, the more you get, directly and indirectly. This may go against conventional wisdom, but it works remarkably well when it comes from genuine service-focused intention.

Searching for a way to be of service requires that you listen at all levels while at the same time thinking about what you have to offer. This places the focus completely on the other person and on what you can give. When you're in a position to give something (and everyone is in that position) you have the power to make someone else's life better. This is exhilarating, and it takes all the pressure off you to be entertaining or witty.

When you give, give without an expectation of getting back. Not from the person you're giving to or anyone else, for that matter. What you offer, whether it's a phone number to a cherished resource or the name of your family chiropractor, it must be given without a demand, implied or stated, that something must be offered in return. Otherwise, it's not a gift. It's coercion. And people can tell the difference.

'No Quid Pro Quo' is the first rule of reciprocity. In *Achieving Success Through Social Capital*, Dr. Wayne Baker explains: "The principle of reciprocity explains why building social capital works: When you use your networks to contribute to others, others contribute to you."

There is an essential difference between offering something freely and offering it with strings, especially when you give something of no value in hopes of getting something of value in return. That's Quid Pro Quo at its worst.

Here's where you return to your real intention. If your intention is to be of service, and it's an authentic intent, then what you offer will be given freely and without strings, and others will sense that and feel free to accept. Does this mean that you shouldn't accept something in return? Not at all. It is important to be clear about what you want and to be open to receiving help. It does mean, however, that your offering doesn't come with a built-in guilt-load so that the recipient feels that he has to give back. When you always have something to offer others (and your resources are indeed immense) and you are looking to make those resources available, you are very powerful indeed. You have the ability to change people's lives for the better in even the shortest of conversations.

List information you need to bring back next week that will help someone in the class.

Week Four

Assignment: List who you know and share your resources (i.e., accountants, attorneys, bankers, landscapers). The more you give, the more you will receive.

Your "social capital" is immense. Social capital is defined as everyone you know in your life, and everything all those people have to offer. You don't have to be an expert, just know one. You don't have to have the knowledge, just know where to find it. And it doesn't have to be work-related. For example, if you've met someone who just moved to town, chances are they're looking for referrals to basic services like a veterinarian or a dentist. If you have good service providers, recommend yours. It takes nothing for you to provide a phone number and an address; chances are they're in your PDA or Calendar. It means a great deal to a newcomer to get a recommendation. That's an easy gift to give.

What happens when you enter a networking event with a primary goal of giving to others your valuable information? First of all, you start looking for opportunities to serve. People will be naturally drawn to you because that's the intention you're expressing. You'll automatically start asking good questions and listening carefully for ways to give something of value. And when you do, and do it freely, people will be surprised – and very grateful.

As stated earlier, be clear about what you want as well. While you shouldn't ask for something that is clearly out of proportion to the conversation you're having or the relationship you've created, be clear about your needs and let others help you. You might mention that you're starting a company and are looking for potential investors. You can then add that you're wondering if this person has any suggestions about where to start your search. This is less confrontational than asking for help directly and if the person has an interest in your company, he will say so. Otherwise you might get a useful idea or referral which might be just as important. Be willing to be helped, especially if you've been of service first.

Remember the **4 Steps to Connecting**:

1st Step - Engage empathically and establish a "win-win" partnership.

2nd Step - Understand the other person by listening empathically first.

3rd Step - Be understood by the other person by clearly communicating your point of view.

4th Step - Discuss the issues logically and rationally to reach agreement.

Learn to graciously give AND receive to make a lasting difference for you and others you connect with.

NETWORKING THOUGHTS By Jim Blasingame

In the 21st century, networking is one of the three most important areas small business owners should focus on, along with employing technology and developing strategic alliances. My definition of networking is actively making professional relationships, developing and maintaining those relationships, and leveraging them for the benefit of all parties.

Examples of networking opportunities are everywhere you turn, especially at Chamber of Commerce events, or any venue likely to be attended by business people and community leaders.

NT #1 – Make eye contact: One of the worst things that can be said about your human interaction skills is that you don't look the person you're talking to in the eye. We should be able to remember the color of the person's eyes that we just met.

NT #2 – More ears - less mouth: This is an old adage, but it's an essential networking thought for most of us. We are more likely to impress someone by our interest in them rather than how interested we think they should be in us.

NT #3 – Smile: Ladies are usually better at this than men. But the smile must be genuine, which can be best accomplished with NT #1.

NT #4 – Deliver a firm handshake: Men are usually better at this than the ladies, but don't turn a handshake into a wrestling match. And guys, when you're shaking the hand of a lady, your networking thought is that it's the opposite of dancing: Let the lady lead. Ladies, that means you should offer your hand first, and give 'em a good squeeze.

NT #5 – Do some research: If there is someone you want to get to know whom you think you might be seeing soon, go to their Web site and look around. If you have a mutual friend, ask them about the person to get a little better understanding of what makes this person tick.

NT #6 – Have your elevator speech ready: Imagine that you get on an elevator with someone who asks you what you do before you ask them. Can you deliver a short, concise, and intuitive response before either of you gets off the elevator?

NT #7 – Successful networking benefits all parties: Reread my definition of networking, with emphasis on the last clause. If you enter any networking opportunity with this attitude, instead of a "What's in it for me?" attitude, your networking ROI will increase exponentially.

Write this on a rock - For maximum return on the time you invest in your business, practice and employ your NTs, especially NT# 7.

Networking is more than Showing Up

Networking To-Do List: Write down your goals and areas you need to work on to improve your networking skills. Select three specific goals that are achievable and measureable.

Non-Stop Networking: Maintaining a Network
By Andrea Nierenberg   January 22, 2009

Networking is a process, one that can create business connections to last a lifetime. As business people, we are constantly developing, building, and cultivating relationships, and the truly smart business person develops contacts that act as his or her advocates.

A gardener tends to his or her flower garden by planting the seeds, watering them, checking in on them, and allowing them time to grow. That's exactly how we can build a "bouquet" of people around us.

The following are networking tips that you can use any time of the year. Follow them, try them out, and see what happens as you progress. Here's the secret to making them work: As you continue to add a new tip, keep practicing the previous tips. When you use them like building blocks, you'll be guaranteed excellent results.

1. Build relationships by immediately thanking those who have referred you. My experience has proven to me that if Tom refers me to someone, I'll call and write that person ASAP. Then I'll go back and thank Tom and let him know that I've made contact and will keep him posted.

2. Networking is about relationships and the results that happen. When you cultivate people into your life, you'll reap reward both professionally and personally. They both take time and are worth it.

3. Make lists. Keep a list of your strengths and skills that you can use to prospect. Review it monthly and update it. They might include: Great follow up, sending personal notes and emails, or having a friendly attitude. Whatever they are, keep improving them.

4. Learn to ask for help. Call a business friend or associate and say, "I need some advice." Then follow up with a short thank you note.

5. Be clear and concise in your approach. Remember the **KISS** method - **K**eep **I**t **S**imple **S**weetheart. Don't waste people's time!

6. Reintroduce yourself to people. People will forget who you are, therefore, let them save face. When you see them, say: "Hi, Bob. I'm Andrea Nierenberg. We met a few weeks ago."

7. Promote yourself and your business. Send your prospects short notes with any newsworthy information pertaining to you and your company.

8. Keep detailed notes about the people you meet. Maintain a record of the date and event and who introduced you, the information you discussed, and what your follow up will be.

9. Nurture your network. Make calls and send notes even when it is not directly business-related. As you stay in touch with people, they will remember you, thus will contact you when a need arises.

10. Each week, call one person with whom you haven't spoken for the past 90 days. Give that person an idea for his or her business, a thought, or a new promotion you might have. It's a way of staying in touch and keeping your face in front of your prospects.

11. Invite people to accompany you to events. Take a prospect to a lecture so that you can discuss it later. Let him or her enjoy an event or party with you so that the connections from these events will begin.

12. Send people articles that may interest them. By sending newspaper or magazine articles, it will let people know that you're thinking of them and their business, even if they are not clients right now.

13. Keep a log when and to whom you've written. Keep them in your computer and include notes on special events, vacations, birthdays, and correspondence.

14. Return every phone call within 24 hours. It's professional and courteous, two qualities which are being lost with all the technological advances.

15. Follow-up notes should have follow-up points. For example, thank people for something specific, introduce a new element to stimulate interest (such as an industry development), and conclude with a 'next step,' such as, "I'll call you again in one week."

16. Become an active and perceptive listener. Tune in, remember what someone else says, and use it in a future conversation. Since we only listen with 25% of our listening capacity, you will definitely have greater networking successes if you increase yours.

17. Learn about successful people and their networking techniques. Jack Welch, the most successful CEO of GE, has written many personal, handwritten notes. I do the same and now feel that I'm in great company.

18. Have a strategy and a plan. It might include a goal of meeting two new people this week, setting up a meeting with them, writing a short note, and then calling them one week later.

19. Devote at least twenty minutes to networking per day. Remember, it's a process. Think of all the prospecting you must do to create a contact that becomes a client. Those twenty minutes could be spent writing three notes, or making three extra phone calls - all for the sole purpose of networking and staying in touch.

20. Reconnect with at least three people a week. Every week call a client or prospect you have not been in touch with for at least three months. The reason for contacting them can range from just wanting to say "Hello" to inviting them to a specific event that will interest them.

21. Offer congratulations. If you hear about someone's personal achievement, send a congratulatory note.

22. Extend a special invitation. If you participate in a Chamber of Commerce or another local organization that sponsors special programs, invite some of your contacts to join you as your guest.

23. Give away information. A note from time to time with some valuable information is a good way to keep in touch. Even something as simple as a newspaper clipping that will be meaningful to someone you know.

Transform ~ Stabilize ~ Grow ~ Innovate

The One-Page Strategic Plan (1-PSP™)

The One-Page Strategic Plan (1-PSP™) was developed by Osmond / Pannell and is a slight alteration of the popular One-Page Game Plan™ coined by L. Gary Boomer of Boomer Consulting. Both are a single-page instrument popular in many organizations because they keep the purpose and direction of the organization in the forefront of an individual's mind. They are generally colorful in appearance to aid in recall but also making them stand out in a stack of papers. Recent conventions encourage lamination to avoid accidental loss or destruction. While laminated pieces may be difficult to throw away, some feel it also makes them a strong candidate for continued use. Although debatable, lamination generally does stand the test of time.

The general concept of the 1-PSP is closely tied to an organization's documented goals. While the goal documents are further detailed with tactics, timeframes, measurements, and results, the 1-PSP summarizes the direction of the goals and ties them directly to the organization's strategic direction. Generally speaking, goal documents may be multiple pages almost entirely in pure text, but the 1-PSP is by design, a single page with colorful geometric designs. The simpler the organization / design, the more likely the content will be remembered which is a primary goal of the 1-PSP.

Components of the 1-PSP can vary according to the situation or area of a business using it, but generally speaking, each contains the following elements:

- Company Name
- Vision
- Strategies
- Objective
- Goal
- Tactic / Due Date

Formatting the elements in a standard design helps shared understanding and quick recall. The design generally appears as follows:

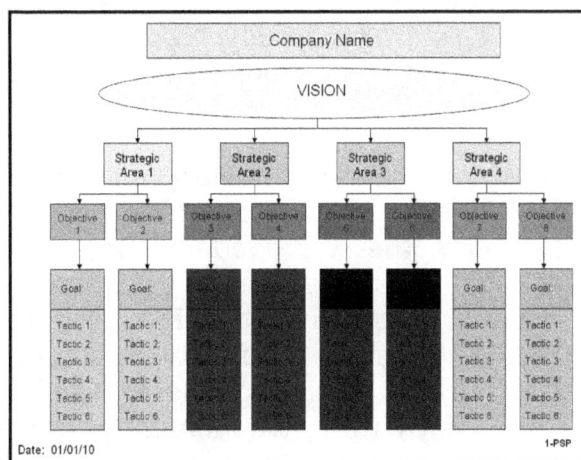

Taking a closer look at each of the element areas, it becomes obvious how the goal and 1-PSP documents relate to one another.

Company Name – This may appear self-explanatory, but the fact is, many organizations either purposely omit their name, citing confidentiality, or they simply fail to place their name on the document. In either event, a Strategic Planning document with no company name at the top is unlikely to be taken seriously by those who are expected to use and follow it. Alternately, some organizations make multiple 1-PSP documents listing the company name at the top and the sub-units or functions directly below. When this is the case, it is not uncommon for the corporate plan to be on one side of the document and the functional plan on the other. On the functional side, however, the function name is listed directly below the corporate name in the same area. This is an excellent way to reinforce how the different areas of the business are working strategically toward the same direction.

Vision – By placing the company's Vision at the top of the document directly under the company name, it brings clarity and eliminates ambiguity to the Strategic Plan. This is an important part of the document and must not be omitted. As was the case earlier, it is not uncommon for sub-units or functions to have their own area Vision Statements which generally align appropriately to the corporate vision. Where this is the case, it would be acceptable to place the functional vision, without the corporate vision, on the functional side of the document.

Strategies – The strategies are the outcome of a business strategy planning session and may adjust slightly over time as the business environments change. They indicate areas where the company feels emphasis must be placed to build or sustain competitive advantage. Quite often these areas are identified through exercises like SWOT (identifying Strengths, Weaknesses, Opportunities and Threats) and TOWS (external Threats, external Opportunities, internal Weakness, and internal Strengths). As strategic components of a competitive advantage, the strategies generally cross functional boundaries and become key elements that bond a company's Strategic Plan. As such, it would be unusual for functional areas not to have identical strategies with the parent company.

Objectives – Objectives describe areas that will be used to support the strategies in building or sustaining a competitive advantage. They are much more specific than the strategies and may or may not cross functional boundaries. In some cultures, Objectives and Goals are terms which are used interchangeably. In the 1-PSP, Objectives serve the purpose of being the overarching category for multiple Goals and Tactics.

Goals – Goals for any substantial Strategic Plan will follow the S.M.A.R.T. convention. Whether the 1-PSP is for the corporate or functional area of the business, the Goals are listed below the corresponding Objective. Where specific Goals are shared across functional lines, the Goal will be documented under each area and generally is marked with an asterisk (*). It is also very important that the language of the Goal is the same across the functional lines. If not, ambiguity can arise and the best result may be a half-completed Goal. For this reason, shared Goals are usually written jointly with management approval before they are finally established.

Tactics / Due Dates – Tactics are the final element of the 1-PSP and make up the majority of space on the document. It is not uncommon for them to take up to one-half of the page. Tactics are very specific and are always ended with the expected completion date or time period in parenthesis. Some organizations find it helpful to put Tactics in chronological order to make it easier to identify at a glance what should be occurring at any given time. However, this may not be an exercise worth the effort considering that there are not an excessive amount of Tactics which can be included on one-half of a page. Furthermore, Tactics and due dates are tracked and measured on the SMART Goal document. A better way to display status of Tactics may be in establishing a dashboard document or high-level summary with red, yellow, and green indicators of status.

The 1-PSP is an extremely important document for any business. Much like its accompanying SMART Goals document, it is a basic building block to building and / or sustaining the success of the business. The attractiveness of design and ease of use functionality make it a powerful tool for any business owner. It can be used to keep everyone in the business literally on the same page and it can demonstrate clear direction when discussing business affairs with bankers, attorneys, accountants, or other business associates.

Smart Goals

Generally speaking, when individuals reference the term "Smart" while simultaneously addressing Goals, they are referring to the acronym S.M.A.R.T. Over time, this acronym has had a variety of definitions, but the most accepted have included the five common characteristics of a Goal. Some would go so far as to say a well-defined Goal can only be a SMART Goal.

The origin of SMART Goals is not known, however, many point to Peter Drucker's 1954 classic titled "The Practice of Management." In his book, there is a reference to similar characteristics where Drucker discusses object-based management. Drucker is not the only person addressing Goals in reference to Objectives. Many individuals familiar with project management are acutely aware of the need to define Objectives in a fashion easily translated to a diverse team working on a particular project. They also have found success in the use of SMART Goals.

The words used to create the acronym have also been widely debated and varied, but again, generally speaking, they have been narrowed down to the following:

S – Specific
M – Measurable
A – Attainable
R – Relevant
T – Time-bound

There is also another acronym used in recent management programs to address goals. This relatively new acronym is known by D.U.M.B.

In this acronym, the terms used to create it are:

D – Doable
U – Understandable
M – Manageable
B – Beneficial

On the surface, the apparent negative connotation of this second acronym could be a turn-off for many individuals, this author concluded. The thought of a need to "dummy-down" a term in order to make it more applicable to areas beyond management and project management are questionable. Therefore, this discussion will continue to expound on only the S.M.A.R.T. acronym.

When defining a Goal, the primary objective should be to answer the following questions: 1) What are we trying to accomplish? 2) How will we know whether or not we are successful? and 3) What is the result if we are not successful? This is where the SMART definitions are the most powerful. Done correctly, they are the guidelines for making sure the Goals are complete when written.

To get a better understanding, the terms or words of the SMART acronym must be defined in more detail.

'S'pecific is the part of the Goal that describes the "What" and the "Why" and the "How" of the Goal. The focus is on the effort and the expectation of the Goal. It has often been said that when a Goal is specific, it is written in a manner in which your grandmother would be able to understand it, regardless of the type of business involved.

An example of a non-specific Goal might be: "Modernize the office."

Ask yourself these three questions – What, Why, and How? If the Goal as written can answer those questions, you are on your way to a Specific Goal. In this example, assumptions could be made as to the answers, but that defeats the purpose. Said another way, there should be no ambiguity when the Goal is written.

A better Goal might be: "Upgrade the reception area at the main office to reflect a positive image and a commitment to security awareness by end of first quarter, 2010."

Again, by asking the three questions, we understand the "What" to be an upgrade of the reception area at the main office. This is very specific and there is no ambiguity. The "Why" is clearly to reflect a positive image and commitment to security awareness. This describes a specific focus for the efforts of this Goal. Finally, the "How" identifies that this Goal is to be completed by a very specific time and date. Can it be finished earlier than the end of the first quarter? Of course it can. However, there is no confusion in that it MUST be completed by a specific date, March 31, 2010.

'M'easurable describes the Tactics, steps, or the approach that will be taken to accomplish the Goal. These are the individual parts that make up the "What" of the Goal and are monitored at the lowest level in the plan to demonstrate whether or not progress is being made towards a successful completion of the Goal. Ultimately, this is the source of success or failure and can be visualized as links in the chain of the process. By applying the old adage, a Goal is only as strong as its weakest link.

Using our same example, a non-measurable Tactic might be: "Modernize the office."

To understand measurable Tactics, ask the question, "What will this Goal look like when it has been completed successfully?" Does the phrase "Modernize the office" look the same to everyone when completed? Hardly! One person might see a new throw rug at the front door. Another may see a completely remodeled area with twice the space! Again, ambiguity with no measurable criteria does not foster success.

The better Goal example was "Upgrade the reception area at the main office to reflect a positive image and a commitment to security awareness by end of first quarter, 2010."

A better Tactic for this goal might be:

1. Research security cameras for the reception area at the main office by 1/15/10.
2. Write RFP for security cameras by 1/20/10.
3. Award contract for security camera installation by 2/10/10.
4. Security cameras installed and working successfully by 3/1/10.
5. Staff trained on the use, response, and support of security cameras by 3/15/10.

Referring back to the Goal, notice that the Tactics above only represent a portion of the Goal. Tactics should be written to address the "positive image" portion of the upgrade. These could include such things as researching architects or interior designers, etc.

'A'ttainable is the part of the Goal which motivates success. This is not to be confused with or used interchangeably with the term "easy." Most of the time, Attainable is slightly out of immediate grasp but not so far out as to be impossible to achieve within given constraints. If a Goal is written which is known to be "easy," it is more likely to be a routine task or a delegable activity. An "Attainable" Goal requires planning and should be expected to be achieved with the support of all functions required to make it successful. Generally, this means the Goal is within the business strategic direction, is fully funded, and has committed resources (personnel, equipment, executive support, etc.). Additionally, this is the area where project management seeks to obtain "buy-in" from project stakeholders.

Using our example, the non-attainable tactic might be: "Modernize the office."

Again, ask the question, "What will the success of this Goal look like?" Some may say, replace the light bulbs and you are done! Others may visualize selling the current plant and building in a foreign country! The ambiguity underscores that the goal as unattainable. If there is any doubt, consider whether or not your grandmother would be able to attain the Goal as written.

The better Goal example was "Upgrade the reception area at the main office to reflect a positive image and a commitment to security awareness by end of first quarter, 2010." To be Attainable, the Goal should be assigned across the multiple functions of the organization which will be, in part, responsible for its success. In this case, Executive Management, Finance, HR, Facilities, and Security, at a minimum, should participate in this as a shared Goal. Additionally, IT, Purchasing and Sales may have a shared interest.

'R'elevant Goals drive a business's mission and its vision. It has often been said that if a Goal is not contributing directly to a business's bottom line, it is not worth pursuing. While a company's bottom line is indeed important, sometimes it is not the only thing worthy of a Goal. For example, it could be said that compliance Goals do not contribute to a firm's bottom line. However, without compliance Goals, a firm could be out of business with a "shut down" order from the governing agency over their activities.

In our example, the non-relevant goal is: "Modernize the office."

The question here is how does this goal improve our business, grow our sales, or make us a better company? More precisely, how does this Goal relate to our Mission? The answer is again unclear. Some may think a modern image will boost sales. Some may think a modernized office will improve employee morale. The ambiguity makes it very confusing.

The better Goal example was "Upgrade the reception area at the main office to reflect a positive image and a commitment to security awareness by end of first quarter, 2010." The Relevance may still be unclear. In order to eliminate all confusion, the Goal must be tied to the company's strategic focus. This is identified on the One-Page Strategic Plan (1-PSP).

'T'ime-bound is exactly as it sounds. This portion of the Goal is very explicit in when the goal is expected to be completed. Although seldom spelled out, it also implies that the Goal will be completed successfully by the time stated. This is often the easiest part in writing a SMART Goal and the most overlooked. It is also why it is a good idea to have others read over the Goals to validate that they are clear, free of ambiguity, and follow the SMART convention.

In our example, the non-time-bound goal is: "Modernize the office."

At first glance, it may appear that this is obviously not Time-bound. However, remember that when writing Goals, it is easy to leave out what may be assumed by others. For example, if it has been clearly announced from top management that in the near future, employees will be seeing evidence of new construction around the plant, the above goal may seem adequate. The truth is that one can never assume anything. Remember, would your grandmother know when the Goal was going to be complete by reading the above statement? Probably not!

The better Goal example was "Upgrade the reception area at the main office to reflect a positive image and a commitment to security awareness by end of first quarter, 2010." Assuming the writing of this Goal is sometime in fourth quarter, 2009 and that work on the Goal is to start January 1, 2010, then on the surface this goal appears Time-bound. The test of being Time-bound is looking into the Tactics discussed earlier. This becomes a part of good project management where the individual steps are planned out in great detail and the timeline is worked backwards to assure successful completion is feasible. If it is not found feasible, then the Goal should be rewritten to fit the appropriate timeframe.

What do SMART Goals look like when they are put together in one document? Here is one way they might be viewed using our current example.

Roadmap – Reaching you Goals through Strategic Measurements

Strategic Area	Objective	Status	Goal	Tactics	When/How Measured	Results	Achieved? Yes/No
OPERATIONS	Perimeter Security	●	Upgrade the reception area at the main office to reflect a positive image and commitment to security awareness by end of first quarter, 2010	1. Research security cameras for the reception area at the main office by 1/15/10	1/15/10 -Interviews with camera vendors complete; internet research completed, documented and analysis prepared; inquiries to security associations received and analyzed; requirements for RFP completed	Security camera research completed	YES
				2. Write RFB for security cameras by 1/20/10	1/18/10 - First draft of RFB completed and submitted for management review; 1/19/10 - RFB revised and submitted for approval; 1/20/10 - RFB written, reviewed, approved and put out to vendors	RFB completed and submitted to vendors	YES
				3. Award contract for security camera installation by 2/10/10	1/25/10 – 4 contract bids received and reviewed; 1/30/10 - 3 contract bids sent for management review; 2/05/10 - 1 contract and 1 backup contract approved by management; 2/10/10 - contract awarded and vendor notified	Contract awarded	YES
				4. Security cameras installed and working successfully by 3/1/10	2/15/10 - Camera installation begins; 2/20/10 - camera testing begins; 2/25/10 - review of camera tapes for issues begins; 2/28/10 - camera installation complete and declared successful by vendor and client management team.	Camera installation complete	YES
				5. Staff trained on the use, response and support of security cameras by 3/15/10	3/3/10 - Security staff trained on camera use, observation and tape maintenance/review; 3/5/10 - Management briefed on camera tape observation and use; 3/10/10 - Reception staff trained on emergency use of cameras and emergency signals to security staff monitoring cameras.	Staff training complete	YES

This is also called the Roadmap because it views the lifecycle of the Goals. In other words, from the highest level of creation, the strategy, through the implementation stage, Tactics. The Roadmap allows displays where and how well progress is being made during the process.

Many times, a "Dashboard" signal is provided on the Roadmap to visually represent any specific Goal's status. Often times, this signal indicates the status of a specific Goal or the Goal of a key performance indicator. The Key Performance Indicator (KPI) is one selected by the management team as one which is critical to the success of the Strategic Plan.

SMART Goals are the basic building blocks to keep a business focused on the activities and efforts necessary for sustainable success. They remove barriers of confusion, direction, and indecisiveness. Once understood and practiced, they become a fundamental part of everyday business. Like any good habit, success breeds continued use.

Case Study – Transforming a Business

How can they transform their business? Identify WHO their customers are and HOW they are going to reach them to grow the business.

How can they continue to grow their business?

Key Point: Never Stop Transforming the Business!

Human Resource Strategies – Explore Insights Discovery®

- Finding the Inner Self
- Understanding Others
- Adapting and Connecting
- Taking Action

How many faces can you find in the picture above?

We each see the world through our own lenses. Those lenses are tinted by our perspective of the world. We have preferences and they are interwoven into our view of the world. The energies we use at any moment in time are dependent on the needs of those around us and our ability to connect with them.

Preferences

Introverted / Extroverted

Definition

Are you energized from within and by yourself or are you energized by associating with others? For example, if you are driving home from work and you just miss being in a car accident, would you go home and lay down in a quiet room to rest or would you call your best friend and tell her all about it?

What colors are Introverted? What colors are Extroverted?

Extroverted – Yellow and Red

Introverted – Blue and Green

Thinking / Feeling

Definition

This is the preference that is the source of much of your analysis and assumptions. Thinking is logical and orderly while Feeling is sensitive to others and considers the not-so-logical impact. For example, if you have been working on a problem and you have the solution, do you say I think I have the answer or I feel that this answer is right?

What colors are Thinking? What colors are Feeling?

Thinking – Blue and Red

Feeling – Green and Yellow

Sensing / Intuitive

Definition

How do you receive information, by your senses or by some internal clock that is hard to identify? For example, if you have to see the hard evidence before you will make up your mind, you are Sensing. If you can imagine the conclusion without seeing all the facts, you are Intuitive.

This preference is not specific to the various colors and can be found to cross all of them.

Insights® Color Energies

Cool Blue - Introverted Thinking / Reflection

As someone with a high level of Cool Blue energy, you are Introverted and have a desire to know and understand the world around you. You like to think before you act and maintain a detached, objective standpoint. You value independence and intellect. You prefer written communication in order to maintain clarity and precision, radiating a desire for analysis.

Earth Green - Introverted Feeling / One-to-One Relationship and Support

As someone with a high level of Earth Green energy, you are Introverted. You focus on values and depth in relationships. You want others to be able to rely on you. You will defend what you value with quiet determination and persistence. You prefer democratic relations that value the individual and are personal in style, radiating a desire for understanding.

Sunshine Yellow - Extroverted Feeling / Articulated Vision and Inspiration

As someone with a high level of Sunshine Yellow energy, you are strongly Extroverted, radiant, and friendly. You are usually positive and concerned with good human relations. You enjoy the company of others and believe that life should be fun. You approach others in a persuasive, democratic manner, radiating a desire for sociability.

Fiery Red - Extroverted Thinking / Assertive Action and Direction

As someone with a high level of Fiery Red energy, you are Extroverted and have high energy. You are action-oriented and always in motion. You are positive, reality-oriented and assertive. You are single-minded as you focus on results and objectives. You approach others in a direct, authoritative manner, radiating a desire for power and control.

Preferences	Red	Yellow	Green	Blue
Appearance	Businesslike	Fashionable	Casual	Formal
	Functional	Stylish	Conforming	Conservative
How they work	Busy	Stimulating	Personal	Structured
	Formal	Personal	Relaxed	Organized
	Efficient	Cluttered	Friendly	Functional
	Structured	Friendly	Informal	Formal

Principles

- ✳ This is not about leadership.
- ✳ We all have ALL four color energies ALL the time.
- ✳ Which color energy we use depends on who we're working with and what we're working on.
- ✳ The focus is on the Individual, not the Type.

Understanding Differences

How can we begin to recognize and value everyone's differences? Our actions and preferences reflect who we are. We can see then recognize the differences!

Preferences	Red	Yellow	Green	Blue
Energies	• Competitive • Demanding • Determined • Strong-Willed • Purposeful • Driver	• Sociable • Dynamic • Demonstra-tive • Enthusiastic • Persuasive • Expressive	• Caring • Encouraging • Sharing • Patient • Relaxed • Amiable	• Cautious • Precise • Deliberate • Questioning • Formal • Analytical
Verbal	• 'Tell' style • Faster pace • Fills silences • Sounds confident • Responds quickly • Spontaneous	• More emo-tional • Animated • Casual • Expressive • Asks personal questions	• 'Ask' style • Slower pace • Quieter speech • Thinks first • Diplomatic • Keeps to self	• Controlled • Little emotion • Monotone • Questioning • Critical & blunt • Nit-picker
Interaction	• Direct • Outgoing • Less patient • Challenges facts • Focus on future	• Relationships • Easy going • Flexible • Friendly & considerate • Small talk • Cooperative	• Indirect • Co-ordinates • Systematic • Little chal-lenge • Moderate	• Task Focus • Punctual • Forthright • Independent • Controlling • Analyses • Evaluates
Body Language	• Leans forward • Full eye contact • Aggressive • Impatient • More ges-tures • Firm handshake	• Open • Responsive • More expression • Physical contact • Relaxed • Social	• Quiet, reserved • Intermittent eye contact • Gentle handshake • Few gestures • Avoids touch • Reserved	• Detached • Less facial expression • No physical contact • Rigid body • Business-like
Stress	• Become impatient • Increase demands • Increase pressure • Go quicker	• Yell • Scream • Throw things • Take things personally	• Self destructive thoughts • Deeply hurt feelings • Ruminating on rights and wrongs	• Withdraw • Try and understand • Split hairs • Wait for certainty • Go quietly

Adapting and Connecting

How do we adapt and connect with other individuals who have color energies in different levels than we do?

Adapting

We change our natural behavior to suit the circumstance or the needs of those around us. Some of us do this naturally and constantly. Many of us THINK we do it naturally and constantly.

We adapt to:

- ♯ Conform
- ♯ Gain approval and acceptance
- ♯ Cooperate with others
- ♯ Treat people the way they like to be treated
- ♯ Get more done – effective and efficient
- ♯ Achieve our goals and objectives

Connecting

Once we learn how to adapt to the preferences of others, we can focus on connecting. We move from blissful ignorance to adapting, then to connecting, and finally to versatility.

Progress

I can work in your comfort zone and make you feel good without thinking about it.

I know what to do and when I work at it I can connect with you.

I realize and accept that you are different.

This is me. Take me or leave me.

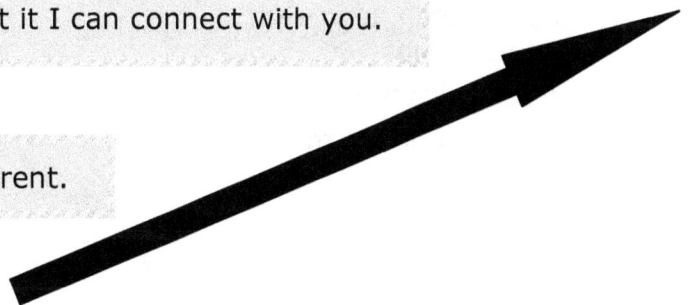

Value our Differences

The basic premise of Insights is ... "We don't want to change you. You are perfect just the way you are – a unique combination of personality, attitudes, and intelligence that will never be repeated. We would like to help you be the best that you can possibly be and achieve all the things you want from life - relationships, success, peace of mind – you can choose." How wonderful that we are all different.

Insight Connections

Cool Blue Energy

STRENGTHS

- Knowledgeable and detailed
- Air of competence
- Asks probing questions
- Thorough follow-up

WEAKNESSES

- Initial interaction may be difficult & stuffy
- Questions may be seen as critical & insensitive
- Overlooks others' feelings
- Focus on inconsequential details

Fiery Red Energy

STRENGTHS

- Confident, determined
- Loves challenges
- Focused
- Influencing others

WEAKNESSES

- Poor listener
- Can be seen as arrogant
- May push too hard
- Doesn't wait for feedback

Earth Green Energy

STRENGTHS

- Builds deep, long-term relationships
- Natural listener
- Sincere and warm
- Persistent

WEAKNESSES

- Slow to adapt
- May lack enthusiasm asking for a decision
- Avoids rejection
- Takes difficulties personally

Sunshine Yellow Energy

STRENGTHS

- Quick to build relationships
- Friendly and sociable
- Adaptable, imaginative
- Skillful presenter

WEAKNESSES

- May lack focus
- Too casual for some
- Poor planning and follow-up
- Can lose interest

Learning Styles – Blue Energy

Learners Who Prefer Blue Energy
- Learn best alone, independent learners
- Need books and materials more than other energy types
- Like quiet, uninterrupted work
- Love to read books
- Self-paced, like to take one thing at a time
- Usually self-motivated
- Value expert knowledge
- Enjoy logical analysis and reasoning

Suggested Learning Strategies
- Carefully organize your learning – make a detailed plan
- Learn from lectures and experts through books
- Analyze your learning – ask why and what if?

The Blue Classroom
- Has a businesslike, orderly atmosphere
- Gives students some control over material learned and schedules
- Uses small group or individual activities
- Uses involved, detailed projects

Learning Styles – Green Energy

Learners Who Prefer Green Energy
- Learn best from instructors they like
- Have concern for fellow classmates
- Appreciate quiet, uninterrupted work
- Sensitive to classroom climate, value social harmony
- Often learn by association, can become interested in areas not directly related to the main topic
- Don't enjoy time-pressured activities
- Prefer learning from people rather than books

Suggested Learning Strategies
- Use a mentor or buddy for guidance
- Adopt review & summary sessions with a friend
- Ask yourself "How is this relevant?"

The Green Classroom
- Uses small group or 'buddy'; cooperative learning
- Is quiet, safe, and warm in climate
- Acknowledges all learners' needs, avoids criticism and respects manners

Learning Styles – Yellow Energy

Learners Who Prefer Yellow Energy
- Like group learning and activities
- Don't learn well by themselves
- High activity levels
- Learning must be fun and enjoyable
- Multimedia, bells, & whistles
- Very interactive & spontaneous
- Multiple people talking and presenting, including themselves
- Can be very imaginative learners

Suggested Learning Strategies
- Use chats, brainstorming, and 'big-picture' planning
- Learn from fun activities and interactive animations & video
- Adopt team exercises or collaboration

The Yellow Classroom
- Has social breaks in the study routine
- Values interaction and group learning
- Has lots of variety and learning aids

Learning Styles – Red Energy

Learners Who Prefer Red Energy
- Need to know what and why they are learning
- Want to be put in charge of projects, or will take charge of projects!
- Get things done well and on time
- Learning needs to be practical and usable
- Like to focus on 'action' rather than 'theory'
- Competitive and can be perceived as bossy
- Like to be in control of their learning

Suggested Learning Strategies
- Use an index or table of contents for self-directed learning
- Give examples and use exercises to practice what you learn
- Use strategies such as step-by-step planning and summaries

The Red Classroom
- Is task orientated, gets the job done
- Allows students to be independent learners
- Is physically and verbally active

Communicating with an Observer

- ₪ Prefers the written word. Documents and reports should contain detailed examination.
- ₪ Expect them to come back to you after the meeting for clarification.
- ₪ Great probers of information and will keep going until they understand fully what is going on.

Do	**Don't**
₪ Be well prepared and thorough	₪ Invade their personal space
₪ Put important things in writing	₪ Be flippant on important issues
₪ Let them consider all the details	₪ Change their routine without notice

Communicating with a Supporter

- ₪ Prefers a slow pace with plenty of quiet time to reflect on issues.
- ₪ Prefers the written word so that they can go away and read it properly.
- ₪ Great listeners but may sometimes give the impression that they are not enthusiastic

Do	**Don't**
₪ Be patient and supportive	₪ Take advantage of their good nature
₪ Slow down and communicate at their pace	₪ Push them to make quick decisions
₪ Ask their opinion and give them time to answer	₪ Spring last-minute surprises

Communicating with an Inspirer

- ₪ Likes enthusiasm and excitement; prefers pictures to text.
- ₪ Tends to finish others' sentences and appear impatient.
- ₪ Not normally good listeners and will become easily distracted.

Do	**Don't**
₪ Be friendly and sociable	₪ Bore them with details
₪ Be entertaining and stimulating	₪ Tie them down with routine
₪ Be open and flexible	₪ Ask them to do it alone

Communicating with a Director

- ₪ Likes the spoken word, confident, and fast paced, i.e., Be brief and be gone.
- ₪ Written documents should be kept brief and concise.
- ₪ Usually not good listeners and may tend to react loudly to things they don't understand.

Do	**Don't**
₪ Be direct and to the point	₪ Hesitate or waffle
₪ Focus on results and objectives	₪ Focus on feelings
₪ Be brief, be bright, and be gone	₪ Try to take over

"The problem with the poor communicator is that the communicator does not know he is not getting across. He can and should know through a combination of feedback and an awareness of others' perceptions, response and body language." - B. Hurst

Blue Dealing with Stress
STRESS CAUSES:
Lack of information, structure & logic
Poor quality work
Time wasted or task rushed
STRESS SIGNALS:
Becomes questioning and deliberate
Nit picking
Aloof, withdrawn, and resentful
REMEDY:
Get feedback on the way forward
Informational and emotional support
Go back to beginning and analyze

Red Dealing with Stress
STRESS CAUSES:
Lack of focus
Indecisiveness
Being out of control
STRESS SIGNALS:
Becomes aggressive
Impatient
Irritable, demanding
REMEDY:
Allow for fast action
Take decisions or time out
Put them in control

Green Dealing with Stress
STRESS CAUSES:
Unfair or impersonal treatment
Violation of values
Interruptions or time pressures
STRESS SIGNALS:
Becomes silent, withdrawn or hurt
Judgmental, impersonal, resistant
Stubborn and over cautious
REMEDY:
Personal contact to restore trust
Understanding sincerity
Put the task aside to another day

Yellow Dealing with Stress
STRESS CAUSES:
Restriction on flexibility
No interaction and fun
Personal rejection
STRESS SIGNALS:
Over responsive
Appears opinionated
Argumentative
REMEDY:
Allow room for maneuvering
Save face
Distract onto something different

Insights® is a global learning and development company working in partnership with leading organizations across the world.

Our transformational learning solutions are supported by our extensive portfolio of customizable products and services. This portfolio, delivered by Insights' worldwide team of exceptional and inspirational people, helps our clients improve their effectiveness in five key areas:
- Individuals
- Teams
- Organizations
- Sales
- Leadership

Underpinning our learning solutions are two unique and complementary learning systems, Discovery and Navigator. These systems measure preference and capability and provide an engaging and accessible language for learning.

This language, threaded through our entire portfolio, enables our clients to experience rich, deep and inspiring learning solutions that enhance relationships, improve performance and change personal and professional lives forever.

Transform ~ **Stabilize** ~ Grow ~ Innovate

Financial Strategies

The owner of a small business is responsible for the success and survival of the company. The business owner is seldom an economic guru or a highly-educated financial expert. Many business owners did not start their business with the intent to make a mark for themselves in the world financial markets or change the course of history through the discovery of a new monetary strategy. The truth is, many small business owners have a great idea for a new product or service and their passion lies in bringing that idea to market to solve a specific problem or answer a need. When they are successful, it is seldom because they set out to become rich overnight! In fact, many a small business owner will quietly confess that the financial side of the business is what they fear the most! They find it confusing, time intensive and frankly … boring! It comes with its own language and it seems that everyone from accountants, CPAs, and bankers, to financial consultants, business analysts and investment brokers has cornered the market on interpreting for the small business owners.

However, if the small business owner is to survive and become successful, it is in their best interest to understand and control the financial health of their company. Many will tell you that they accomplish this understanding and control through a gut instinct that tells them when the business is heading in the wrong direction or sliding into uncharted territory. The problem with gut instincts is that if one is focused on an immediate need, the instinct can fall second or third to that need. If the gut instinct is on target, by the time the business owner gets around to acting on that instinct, it may be too late. But it does not take a Masters in Finance to understand the basic financial reports for business survival and ultimate success for the small business owner. What follows is a basic overview for a Finance 101 understanding and the foundation necessary for speaking the language or interpreting the recommendations from the experts.

Basic Financial Statements

"When I want to understand what is happening today, I try to decide what will happen tomorrow; I look back; a page of history is worth a volume of logic."
Oliver Wendell Holmes

Oliver Wendell Holmes (1809-1894) - US author & physician; wrote essay collection "The Autocrat of the Breakfast-Table" 1857, poems "Old Ironsides" "The Chambered Nautilus" "The Deacon's Masterpiece, or, the Wonderful One-Hoss Shay"[1]

Business starts with resources. Those resources may be in the form of cash from the owner, loans from the bank or friends, or the sale of stock for an interest in the business. The resources also may be in the form of real estate, equipment, supplies, fixtures or other items necessary for conducting the business.

---

[1] BookRags (2009) Oliver Wendell Holmes, Sr. Retrieved on 2/27/2009 from: http://www.bookrags.com/Oliver_Wendell_Holmes,_Sr.

The business owner is held accountable for obtaining, using, tracking, and reporting where those resources are and how they are being utilized. The basic financial statements are one way of accomplishing this task. The Balance Sheet, Income Statement and Cash Flow Statement demonstrate the past use of resources at a given point in time. Most generally, they are prepared on an annual or quarterly basis, although depending on the size of the business, they may be prepared as often as monthly. The Balance Sheet and Income Statement will be examined in greater detail below. The Cash Flow Statement will be discussed later.

The Balance Sheet

The Balance Sheet is also known at the statement of financial position. This is appropriate since it represents a summary of the fiscal situation for a business at a specific point in time. The Balance Sheet consists of three parts: Assets, Liabilities, and Owners' Equity. A mathematical equation exists between the three parts and can be stated in different ways lending itself to the document's name...Balance Sheet. The most common equation is:

$$\textbf{Assets = Liabilities + Owners' Equity}$$

With the Assets listed on the left side of the documents, the Liabilities and Owners' Equity are listed on the right side. A total at the bottom of the document will demonstrate that the total amount of Assets is exactly equal to the total of Liabilities added to the total Ownership Equity. Therefore, the information "balances." Another way of expressing the equation is:

$$\textbf{Assets – Liabilities = Owners' Equity}$$

This is one way to calculate the sometimes subjective part of the equation, Owners' Equity. However, the Balance Sheet is generally displayed with the Assets on the left or top of the document and the Liabilities and Owners' Equity on the right or below the Assets.

The contents of the different portions of the Balance Sheet are listed under each of the three parts. For example, on a Small Business Balance Sheet, Assets would be separated between current assets and fixed assets. Current assets might include such items as cash in the bank, accounts receivable, and inventory. Fixed assets are things like real estate and equipment. On the other side of the Balance Sheet, items listed under Liabilities might include accounts payable, long-term notes and accrued expenses like insurance premiums. Also on this side of the Balance Sheet are the contributions to the Owners' Equity which as stated above is the difference between the total assets and the total liabilities.

Sample Small Business Balance Sheet[2]

Assets		Liabilities and Owners' Equity		
Cash	$6,600	**Liabilities**		
Accounts Receivable	$6,200	Notes Payable	$30,000	
		Accounts Payable		
		Total liabilities		$30,000
Tools and equipment	$25,000	**Owners' equity**		
		Capital Stock	$7,000	
		Retained Earnings	$800	
		Total owners' equity		$7,800
Total	$37,800	Total		$37,800

At a glance, the Balance Sheet can answer the questions of relationship like does the business own more than it owes and is there more short-term debt or long-term debt? It also demonstrates what contributions to the business the owner has supplied. The most important point to remember is that this is still just a snapshot in time. The Balance Sheet demonstrates what "was" and not what "is." A new purchase of expensive equipment tomorrow can change the distribution of the Balance Sheet.

The Income Statement

The Income Statement is sometimes called the Profit and Loss Report because it identifies the profitability of the business during a period of time. An important difference between the Balance Sheet and the Income Statement is in the time-frame in which each is reporting. Remember that the Balance Sheet is a snapshot at a particular point in time, usually a specific date like December 31, 2008. The Income Statement, on the other hand, is a period of time and is stated as, "For the Three Months Ending June 30, 2007" which would mean the period of April 1, 2007 through June 30, 2007. In another example, the Income Statement might state "For the Month Ending January 31, 2006" which would mean the period of January 1, 2006, through January 31, 2006.

---

[2] Williams, Jan R.; Susan F. Haka, Mark S. Bettner, Joseph V. Carcello (2008). *Financial & Managerial Accounting*. McGraw-Hill Irwin. pp. 50.

The major content of the Income Statement is important as it lists the revenues, expenses, gains, and losses. The revenues are the proceeds that are realized from the sale of a product or service and sometimes referred to as Income. From this amount, Expenses are subtracted which leaves the business with a gain or loss for that period of time.

Revenues – Expenses = Net Income

Therefore, the Income Statement measures the profit or loss a business experienced. Generally speaking, the Income Statement will include the major items of Revenues, Cost of Goods Sold, Gross Profit Margin, Selling and Administrative Expense, Interest Expense and Taxes.

When examining the operating expenses of a business, two items may surface that require a closer look: Depreciation and Amortization, which are important components. Depreciation refers to an amount of money that is recognized every year of an item's useful life. For example, we depreciate the cost of equipment over time. If an oven for a baker cost $1000 and is expected to last 10 years, then each year, $1000 is depreciated for the next 10 years. Depreciation is taken on capital equipment and tangible assets. Amortization also represents a decline in value but relates to intangible assets such as patents, copyrights, trademarks, and goodwill. Like Depreciation, Amortization allocates the costs of these intangible assets over their useful life.

Additionally, two acronyms are common on the Income Statement and they are: EBIT and EBITDA. EBIT stands for Earnings Before Interest and Taxes. It is often referred to as Operating Income and is calculated by subtracting Operating Costs from Sales Revenue.

EBIT = Sales Revenues – Operating Costs

EBITDA stands for Earnings Before Interest, Taxes, Depreciation and Amortization. Depreciation and Amortization are not cash expenses even though they are reported as costs on the Income Statement. The cash was spent at the time of the purchase. However, it is important to see how much cash is being generated by a company by accounting for the Depreciation and Amortization costs and that is why EBITDA is calculated.

Success in business is often a measurement of profit or net income. The Income Statement demonstrates that as revenue goes up, so does profit. However, when expenses go up, profits go down! This means that success is managed by selling as much as possible while keeping the expenses as low as possible.

Sample Income Statement for a fictitious business

Income Statement for Legal Researchers
For the year ended December 31, 2008

Revenues
GROSS PROFIT (including rental income) $487,153

Expenses:

ACCOUNTING	$8,425
ADVERTISING	3,521
BANK FEES	398
EMPLOYEES	93,500
FRANCHISE FEES	15,775
INSURANCE	9,855
PRINTING	3,500
PROFESSIONAL SERVICES	9,400
RENT	25,450
SUBSCRIPTIONS	589
UTILITIES	11,637

Operating Expenses	$182,050
Earnings before interest, taxes, depreciation and amortization (EBITDA)	305,103
Depreciation & Amortization	38,657
Earnings before interest and taxes (EBIT)	$266,446
Interest and Taxes	27,956
NET INCOME	$238,490

Caution is advised when preparing and examining the Income Statement of a business because there are different ways of calculating the information displayed. For example, Depreciation and Inventory can be calculating in at least two different ways that can impact Net Income. An interesting case in point was reported in *The Wall Street Journal* on April 7, 1993, relating to IBM.[3]

"The changes in IBM's accounting practice fell into three broad categories. The first involved revenue recognition and determining when a sale was actually complete. While some high-technology companies wait until a system is installed and running at a customer site, IBM chose to book revenue upon shipment.[4] In some cases, but only when installation at a customer was expected within 30 days, it even booked shipments to its own warehouses as sales. Another revenue issue was how to account for various sales gimmicks that offered customers liberal return policies or price protection refunds if prices later fell. IBM critics contend that full revenue was being booked at shipment, despite evidence that payments received would be less.

The second category was the treatment of leases. Many of IBM's leases had revenue streams that fell short of GAAP requirements for capital leases. Instead of qualifying as sales when the contract was signed, with all the expected revenue booked at once, they would have to be treated as rentals, with the revenue only booked as payments were received. In an extremely unusual transaction, IBM purchases insurance that guaranteed the value of the computers at the end of the lease. This residual value, when added to the payments from the customer, met the GAAP tests and allowed IBM to recognize the sales immediately.

Finally, starting in 1984, IBM began to reduce the estimated cost of its retirement plans and to spread the costs of its factories further into the future. Though these changes were fully disclosed in IBM's Financial Statements and were common at other companies, critics maintained they were a shift away from IBM's traditionally conservative accounting."

---

[3] Michael W. Miller and Lee Berton, "As IBM's Woes Grew, It Accounting Tactics Got Less Conservative," *The Wall Street Journal*, April 1993, p.1.

[4] In 1987, the SEC filed suit against another computer manufacturer, Storage Technology Corp., for recognizing revenue when product was shipped rather than installed. The SEC also charged that a major transaction had been backdated in 1983 to turn a loss into a profit. The suit was settled with no admission of wrongdoing.

Budgets

> *"A budget tells us what we can't afford, but it doesn't keep us from buying it."*
> *William Feather*
>
> William Feather (1889 – 1981) was an American publisher and author, based in Cleveland, Ohio.[5]

Budgets or the budgeting process practiced by small businesses is often referred to as a necessary evil and oftentimes brings about a series of low groans from those individuals assigned to the task.

While many tasks listed under the Accounting or Financial umbrella are viewed as boring, the Budget exercise, when properly explained, can become one of the most interesting and exciting aspects of any small business. Previously, it was noted that the Balance Sheet and Income Statements are documents reflecting a business at a specific point of time. Said another way, these are historical references. The Budget, on the other hand, is a document of the current situation demonstrated by measuring a projected allotment against what was actually expended.

The purpose of the small business Budget is two-fold. First, it is a forecast of the income and expenses expected based on the Business Plan. Second, it is a documented account of how the business performed based on that forecast. As such, the Budget is a control tool for managing the day-to-day activities of the business. Additionally, to be more effective and where possible, consider a Budget that:

a) Reflects the reality of the business
   (Line items should identify the needs, wants and nice-to-haves of the business in that order.)

b) Connects accurately from one period to the next
   (Positive and negative balances of a prior period should be reflected in the current period.)

c) Tracks all of the funds
   (Use zero-based budgeting to allocate every item.)

A small business Budget is generally created once a year, but may be reviewed monthly, quarterly, or even semi-annually. Quite often the Budget is reviewed first when financial decisions are required as a means of assessing the business's current fiscal position. Management and sometimes employees are granted limits on expenditures without seeking prior approval based on the portions of the business Budget they control.

Budgets are often a measure of performance, both for a company and for the management team. This can be a true balancing act that should not be taken lightly.

When managers feel they are constrained by a Budget, they had no input into, they will be prone to manipulate the results, putting themselves in the best light. The better approach is allowing management and employees a voice in creating

---

[5] Wikipedia. (2009) William A. Feather. Retrieved on 2/27/2009 from:
http://en.wikipedia.org/wiki/William_Feather

the Budget. Performance can be measured not only on how well they adhered to the Budget but also in how well they adjust to changes in the business and apply those changes appropriately to the Budget. In this way, the Budget becomes a living document that works towards the fundamental success and survival of the business.

The small business Budget generally identifies expected Income and Expense amounts for a specified line item in one column and the corresponding actual amounts in the next column. Sometimes a third column is created that displays the difference between the two amounts. This is called the Variance. The Variance may be a positive number or a negative number depicting whether a particular line item is over/under Budget.

A popular form of budgeting is called the "Zero-Based Budget" which means that every dollar of income is identified with specific expense causing the sum of incomes to be equal to the sum of expenses.

There are a variety of types of budgets that can be used by a small business.

These include but are not limited to:

- Sales Budget
- Inventory Budget
- Production Budget
- Cash Budget
- Marketing Budget
- Project Budget

At the end of the day, the Budget is the business document that tells the small business owner whether they are going in the direction they intended. It puts the small business owner in control of the finances rather than the finances controlling the business. Most of all, it allows for goals to be met and financial crisis to be averted and that means that the business owner can get a good night's sleep!

Sample Budget for a small business

Widget Manufacturing Company
Budget
January 1, 2007 to December 31, 2007

Category	Actual	Budget	Variance (over) /under
Inflows			
Net Sales	385,400	300,000	(85,400)
Cost of Goods			
Merchandise Inventory, January 1	160,000	160,000	0
Purchases	120,000	90,000	(30,000)
Freight Charges	2,500	2,000	(500)
Total Merchandise Handled	282,500	252,000	(30,500)
Less Inventory, December 31	100,000	120,000	20,000
Cost of Goods Sold	182,500	132,000	(50,500)
Gross Profit	202,900	168,000	(34,900)
Interest Income	500	700	200
Total Income	**202,500**	**168,700**	(33,800)
Expenses			
Salaries	68,250	45,000	(23,250)
Utilities	5,800	4,500	(1,300)
Rent	23,000	23,000	0
Office Supplies	2,250	3,000	750
Insurance	3,900	3,900	0
Advertising	8,650	9,000	350
Telephone	2,700	2,300	(400)
Travel and Entertainment	2,550	2,000	(550)
Dues & Subscriptions	1,100	1,000	(100)
Interest Paid	2,140	2,500	360
Repairs & Maintenance	1,250	1,000	(250)
Taxes & Licenses	11,700	10,000	(1,700)
Total Expenses	**133,290**	**106,850**	(26,440)
Net Income	**$69,210**	**$61,850**	(7,360)

Cash Flow Management

"Increased borrowing must be matched by increased ability to repay. Otherwise we aren't expanding the economy, we're merely puffing it up." Henry C. Alexander

Henry C. Alexander (1902 – 1969) Alexander changed the way in which the Morgan Bank did business. Before Alexander, the Morgan Bank did not solicit business. Alexander used greater aggressiveness in the development of new business by training a new generation of employees, known as "bird dogs," to pursue business that had previously come in by itself. His greatest achievement was the merger of JP Morgan with the Guaranty Bank. Prior to the merger, Alexander served as the chief executive of JP Morgan & Company from 1950-1959.[6]

Cash Flow Management has been described as many things including the process of monitoring, analyzing and dealing with the small business cash flows. According to a December 11, 2003, article in *Growing Your Business*, "...cash flow management means delaying outlays of cash as long as possible while encouraging anyone who owes you money to pay it as rapidly as possible."[7] This is certainly true during a down economy, but also holds true for any small business owner with their sights set on growing their business. While growth will be easier for any business with a zero to low debt ratio, many small business owners might well be advised to manage their company finances through an effective Cash Flow Plan.

Planning and managing Cash Flow helps the small business owner prepare, monitor and execute good business decisions based on the money coming in and going out of the business. One way to accomplish the task is to pay close attention to four basic areas: 1) Cash Flow Plan; 2) Receivables Under the Microscope; 3) Control the Payables; and 4) Accrue for Murphy.

Cash Flow Plan

A Cash Flow Plan is much like a Budget but generally is viewed over a greater period of time and demonstrates anticipated highs and lows of the cash required to run the business. It is a forward or future view of the anticipated movement of funds in a business. Information is gathered from all parts of the business to validate the numbers on the plan. Notes or references to documents should be included, especially when information provided is not generally well known or is an infrequent occurrence.

Some information will be easily documented such as fixed payables and receivables. Other data will be more subjective like the varied costs of operations or anticipated sales revenues.

---

[6]Harvard Business School Leadership Database. (2009). "Henry C. Alexander". Retrieved on 2/27/2009 from: http://www.hbs.edu/leadership/database/leaders/henry_c_alexander.html

[7]Growing Your Business (December 11, 2003). "How To Better Manage Your Cash Flow". Entreprenuer.com. Retrieved 3/4/2008 from:
http://www.entrepreneur.com/money/moneymanagement/managingcashflow/article66008.html

It is very important that the subjective data be as accurate as possible or there is no value in the Cash Flow Plan. Many experts consider the Cash Flow Plan as important to a business as their Strategic Plan and Mission Statement. When preparing the Cash Flow Plan, special attention is focused on funds coming into and out of a business over a future period of time. Additionally, this is where attention is placed on the probability of unforeseen occurrences.

Receivables Under the Microscope

Accounts Receivables is one of those items that really looks good on paper, but masks an incredible power to bring a business to its knees or worse! The term "Cash is King" goes a long way to loosen the grip and put the power to grow back in the hands of the small business owner. Businesses that run on cash sales or credit card only, tend to enjoy more opportunities for growth, especially when paired with a well established Cash Flow Plan. For businesses that are suffering from slow paying customers, consider cutting losses by offering a discount on balance if paid immediately. Of course, it goes without saying that credit should be cut off and buying limited to cash only.

Receivables should be managed tightly. This means that credit customers should be billed quickly, offered discounts for early payment, accrue penalties from late payment and should not be allowed to go indefinitely without paying. This includes the ability to continuing purchasing when past purchases have over-due payments! Collection services may be an alternative, but sometimes it is best to take a write-off and cancel the customer's credit.

In addition to examining Receivables, check on old inventory. Inventory which is not moving and has been paid for in full is still costing the company money in terms of space and possibly shelf-life. Identify ways to move the inventory and bring cash into the business. Many small business owners utilize "end-of-year" sales or off-season price reductions to attract cost-conscience customers.

Control the Payables

Just as Receivables must be managed, so must the Payables of the business. However, this is the flip side of the situation. Examine the terms of the Payables to vendors. It may be beneficial to take advantage of discounts for cash payments especially where the item has been ordered and payment received from customers. Sometimes, when supplies or materials have been purchased but are still "work-in-process," payment terms should not be paid until due. In this case, the cash of the business is working longer and harder for the small business owner than for the vendor. Electronic payments to vendors should be made at the last possible day for the same reason. It is important to remember, payments should always be on time and not late. This keeps the small business owner in good standing and provides leverage if necessary in the future for requesting extensions.

Accrue for Murphy

Have you ever heard the saying, "Murphy's Law"? It is a fact of life and business that unexpected things happen at the most inopportune times. The Cash Flow Plan can be utilized as a strategic instrument to counteract this phenomenon. By Accruing set amounts or percentages of amounts in the Cash Flow Plan, funds will be available to offset the unexpected. Even if the unexpected event is more than the funds Accrued, the small business owner is in a better position by having more alternatives. For example, if no funds have been Accrued, the unexpected event may force the cutting of employees, the sale of a business line or even the close of the business. On the other hand, with some Accrued funds, the business owner may be able to approach a family member, friend, banker, or investor with a short-term solution based on their ability to provide a portion of the cash required instead of a physical asset put up as collateral. In tough times, a business owner that demonstrates their ability to plan for the unexpected will always be more credit worthy than one that runs a business without a back-up plan.

The Cash Flow Statement

As was mentioned earlier, the Cash Flow Statement is one of the basic financial statements and as such provides a historic view of the business's Cash Flow. When examining the format of the Cash Flow Statement, it is important to understand that it is different from the other financial statements in that it does not include the amount of future cash that has been recorded on credit. For example, cash sales and credit sales are both on the Balance Sheet and Income Statement. The Cash Flow Statement looks at three specific areas of the business where the cash is generated. Specifically, it identifies operations, investing, and financing. Changes are reflected based on whether the cash is flowing in or out of the business. Operations are related to the products and/or services of the business. Investing typically deals with equipment, assets and investment opportunities. The financing portion is associated with debts, loans & dividends. Below is a sample Cash Flow Statement for a fictitious company:

Cash Flow Statement Steve's Motor Repair and Sales For Year Ended December 31, 2008	
Cash Flow From Operations	
Net Earnings	3,500,000
Additions to Cash	
Depreciation	35,000
Decrease in Accounts Receivable	47,000
Increase in Accounts Payable	43,000
Increase in Taxes Payable	9,650
Subtractions From Cash	
Increase in Inventory	35,000
Net Cash from Operations	3,669,650
Cash Flow From Investing	
Equipment	(670,000)
Cash Flow From Financing	
Notes Payable	35,200
Cash Flow for Year Ended December 31, 2008	3,034,850

Checks and Balances

"What has not been examined impartially has not been well examined. Skepticism is therefore the first step toward truth." Denis Diderot

Denis Diderot (1713 – 1784) French man of letters and philosopher who, from 1745 to 1772, served as chief editor of the *Encyclopédie,* one of the principal works of the Age of Enlightenment.[8]

When checks and balances are in place, a small business owner can feel more at ease that the business is running as intended. However, control over those checks and balances must be observed on a regular basis, i.e., audits and verifications. The Sarbanes-Oxley Act of 2002 identified the importance of internal financial controls in minimizing fraud and abuse.

The intent of financial controls is to ensure timely information whether that information comes from manual or automated systems. The impetus of internal financial controls is the accuracy of transactions. An internal control system consists of several activities, techniques and concepts but is not complex or difficult to implement. The small business owner will rest easier when steps have been taken to avoid predictable pitfalls.

The basic model for protecting a business through internal controls would include but is not necessarily limited to the following: Segregation of duties; Physical controls; Reconciliations; Self-Interest; Control numbers; Delegation authority; Maintaining controls; Audits.

Segregation of Duties

Segregation of duties means to separate authorizations, custody and record keeping tasks in order to limit the amount of risk posed by fraud or error. For example, someone who is responsible for writing checks should not be able to sign the check or reconcile the bank statements. Customer payments which are received in the mail should to the bank or be opened and totaled by someone different than the person responsible for posting payments to the journals or computer system.

Physical Controls

Physical control means tight control for access to business assets. The most common example is locking up the checkbook in a safe with only one or two individuals having the key or combination to retrieve it. Another good example is inventory. Inventory is generally placed in a locked or controlled environment with log sheets showing who retrieved what, when, and how much. Quite often the log will identify not only the persons receiving the materials but also the persons who authorized the distribution of the inventory from the storage area.

---

[8] Wikipedia (2009). Denis Diderot. Retrieved on 2/26/2009 from: http://en.wikipedia.org/wiki/Dennis_Diderot

Generally, most small business also maintain identifying marks, labels or stickers on major business assets like computer systems, vehicles, equipment, and office furniture.

In recent years, more small businesses are protecting assets with security systems which might include cameras, armed guards, and audible alarms.

Reconciliations

Reconciliations are important for internal financial controls. Not only do they provide timely and accurate information to identify any potential errors, but the data are often necessary for business decisions. The growth, success and survival of any small business are all dependent upon having them.

Examples of Reconciliations include:

- monthly bank statements reconciled with the checkbook;
- accounts payable and receivable ledger balances reconciled to detailed aging reports;
- inventory of supplies and materials reconciled to shipping receipts;
- fixed assets reconciled to depreciation schedules;
- vendor payable balances reconciled to statements received; and
- long-term notes or accrued liabilities journals reconciled against billings and statements.

Generally, these items are managed through the monthly close process and records of the close maintained in a separate locked area.

Self-Interest

Self-Interest refers to individuals acting in their own best interest. For example, few people are likely to alert the clerk at the register if an item is omitted from their bill. However, those same people will be the first to inform a merchant that they have been charged for an item they did not order. This concept is important to recognize for small business owners because in the area of financial controls it is an important motivator. If an inventory clerk's pay is tied to shortages and overages in inventory, they are going to be more meticulous in overseeing the accuracy of what moves in and out of inventory. Another example of how well this concept is recognized is when employees are not paid for business expenses they incur until providing documented receipts.

Control Numbers

Control Numbers assure that transactions are not lost or allowed to slip through cracks. It is also a very helpful way of cross-referencing them. Many automated accounting systems provide this functionality as a way of tracking items through various accounting components. Control Numbers and logs are one of the most useful ways of reconciling differences, finding the source of errors and recognizing how to correct process problems. The most common examples of Control Numbers and logs are checks and the checkbook register. Another common use is invoice numbers.

Delegation Authority

Delegation Authority is another good financial control measure. This means that there is a clearly-stated policy in place which identifies who has authority to approve and perform specific actions. It is much like Segregation of Duties, but generally refers to approval on dollar amounts.

For example, first line supervisors may have the authority to approve supply orders up to $500. Managers may have authority to approve various purchasing decisions up to $5000. Amounts over $5000 may require an officer and/or the owner's approval based on the item. Keep in mind that authorization levels should include non-cash items such as purchase returns to avoid bottlenecks in the process.

Maintaining Controls

It is important that the processes and control for financial systems have the utmost integrity. If a system is perceived to be faulty, individuals will begin to work around the system and this opens the door to various kinds of errors and especially fraud. Maintaining controls means validating/verifying the systems are working as designed and assuring that employees are trained and updated on changes in the process. The biggest mistake small businesses make is thinking that short-cuts can be taken on controls and not following the processes established. The fallacy of this reasoning leads to more work in identifying errors on the backend. The fact is that the more attention and planning that goes into controlling the systems on the frontend, speeds up the process for delivering timely and accurate data.

Audits

Audits are the cornerstone of any internal financial controls. They are not to be confused with searching for fraud, but rather for providing assurance that the data delivered via the financial systems is indeed, accurate. When fraud is suspected, experts such as forensic accountants should be contacted to address the issues. Standard audits of systems may be conducted at routine intervals by CPAs and by internal personnel. The results of audits should be reviewed for recommendations and actions implemented where appropriate.

As identified above, Internal Controls are the basis for timely and accurate financial reporting. Additionally, these controls guard against loss and errors. While not all controls are cost-effective, the small business owner must weigh the risk with the rewards and judge for themselves where their comfort level exists. Sources for evaluating the appropriate controls for any business can be found by asking the experts: CPAs, Information Technology Security Analysts, Attorneys, Bankers, and Insurance Agents.

Financial Management

Financial Management is the process by which business owners and managers maximize the value of their business. Throughout this section, attention has been paid to simplifying much of the complex nature of this process. In addition to the methods described previously, Financial Management can also be examined through the use of several financial ratios. They are listed below in no particular order.

Liquidity

Liquidity ratios indicate the relationship of the company's cash and current assets to its current liabilities.

The **Current Ratio** is the primary Liquidity Ratio and is calculated by dividing Current Assets (including cash) by Current Liabilities.

$$\text{Current Ratio} = \frac{\text{Current Assets}}{\text{Current Liabilities}}$$	When a business is in financial difficulty, it may begin paying bills slowly. If current liabilities rise faster than current assets, the current ratio will fall and can be a sign of trouble.

The **Quick Ratio** is another Liquidity Ratio and probably the second most known. It is also known as the acid test. This ratio is calculated by deducting Inventories from Current Assets and dividing the result by Current Liabilities.

$$\text{Quick Ratio} = \frac{\text{Current Assets - Inventories}}{\text{Current Liabilities}}$$	If a business is going to liquidate, inventories are the least liquid and will result in losses. This ratio measures the firms ability to pay off short-term debt without relying on the sale of its inventory.

Asset Management

The **Inventory Turnover Ratio** is one way to measure how effective the business manages its assets, specifically Inventory. In other words, does the Inventory stay in stock for long periods of time or is it sold quickly after receipt? Inventory Turnover is calculated by dividing Sales by Inventories.

$$\text{Inventory Turnover} = \frac{\text{Sales}}{\text{Inventories}}$$	When a business holds onto inventory for long times, this ratio will be low (especially when compared to the industry average). The higher the ratio, the quicker the inventory is selling.

The **Days Sales Outstanding** (DSO) is a measure used to determine how long it takes a business to collect on a sale. This is calculated by dividing the amount of Accounts Receivable by the Average Daily Sales and will result in the number of days that the sales are in Receivables.

$$\text{Days Sales Outstanding} = \frac{\text{Receivables}}{\text{Annual sales / 365}}$$	The higher the number of days sales are outstanding, the longer the company must go without the cash due from the sales. This indicates slow paying customers and reduces the amount of available funds for company use.

The **Fixed Assets Turnover Ratio** indicates how well a company uses its plant and equipment. This ratio is calculated by dividing Sales by Net Fixed Assets.

$$\text{Fixed Assets Turnover} = \frac{\text{Sales}}{\text{Net Fixed Assets}}$$	A low ratio indicates effective use of fixed assets. This ratio should be compared to the company's industry average to identify of how effective they run their business.

Total Assets Turnover Ratio is the final asset management ratio and measures the effective use of all assets owned by the business. It is calculated by dividing Sales by Total Assets.

$$\text{Total Assets Turnover} = \frac{\text{Sales}}{\text{Total Assets}}$$	When a business is not utilizing assets effectively, this ratio will be low compared to the industry average. A low ratio can be managed by increasing sales and/or disposing of assets.

Debt Management

The ratio of Total Debt to Total Assets is often called the *Debt Ratio* and demonstrates the amount of funding provided by creditors. The Debt Ratio is calculated by dividing Total Debt by Total Assets.

$$\text{Debt Ratio} = \frac{\text{Total Debt}}{\text{Total Assets}}$$	A high debt ratio indicates a business that is carrying a relatively high amount of debt. This could make it difficult to obtain additional funding. A business running a low debt ratio is typically funding growth through operations and indicates efficient management practices.

The **Times-Interest-Earned** (TIE) *Ratio* demonstrates how much operating income can fall before a company cannot meet its annual interest costs. The TIE Ratio is calculated by dividing Earnings Before Interest and Taxes (EBIT) by the Interest Charges.

$$\text{TIE Ratio} = \frac{\text{EBIT}}{\text{Interest Charges}}$$	This ratio should be compared to the industry average for the company. If the ratio is lower than the average, it may indicate a potential problem for the business to cover their interest payments. This could lead to legal action and potentially bankruptcy.

The **EBITDA Coverage Ratio** is a comparison of cash flow against financial charges. It is calculated by dividing all cash flows available to meeting fixed financial charges by all fixed financial charges.

EBITDA Coverage = ratio $\dfrac{\text{EBITDA + Lease Payments}}{\text{Interest + Principal Payments + Lease Payments}}$	A ratio lower than the industry average will indicate a business with a relatively high level of debt. This could indicate a business in potential trouble.

Profitability

The **Profitability Ratios** depict the net result of all the financing policies and operating decisions of a business. The *Profit Margin on Sales* identifies the profit per dollar of sales and is calculated by dividing Net Income by Sales.

Profit Margin on Sales = $\dfrac{\text{Net Income}}{\text{Sales}}$	This ratio indicates the efficiency of operations. A low ratio, as compared to the industry average, may be a flag that costs are too high. A low profit margin is also an indicator of high debt.

The **Return on Total Assets Ratio** is a measure of income compared to assets. It is calculated by dividing Net Income by Total Assets.

Return on Total Assets = $\dfrac{\text{Net Income}}{\text{Total Assets}}$	A low ratio below the industry average is generally not good as it is an indicator of high debt. However, this is not always a bad sign especially if a conscious decision has been made to acquire debt. Multiple ratios should be examined before jumping to any conclusions.

The **Basic Earning Power (BEP) Ratio** identifies a business's ability for assets to generate operating income. It is calculated by dividing Earnings before Interest and Taxes by Total Assets.

BEP Ratio = $\dfrac{\text{EBIT}}{\text{Total Assets}}$	This ratio shows the raw earning power of a company's assets. A low ratio as compared to the industry average can indicate a low return on assets.

The **Return on Common Equity (ROE) Ratio** is often considered the "bottom-line" accounting ratio. It is calculated by dividing the Net Income by the Common Equity.

ROE Ratio = $\dfrac{\text{Net Income}}{\text{Common Equity}}$	This ratio is a measure of the rate of return on common stockholders' investment. A lower than industry average may not attract future investor or keep current ones. Additionally, this ratio should be compared to the return on total assets in order to judge the true picture. A ROE ratio higher than a Return on Total Assets ratio may indicate a higher use of debt and is not necessary a negative indicator.

The **Return on Investment (ROI) Ratio** indicates Cash Flow from an investment over a specified period of time, usually a year. ROI is calculated by dividing the Net Income by the Common Equity.

ROI Ratio = $\dfrac{\text{Gains} - \text{Investment Costs}}{\text{Investment Costs}}$	This ratio is a measure of cash generated or lost due to an investment. Other things being equal, the investment with the higher ROI is the better investment. The return on investment metric itself, however, says nothing about the magnitude of returns or risks in the investment.

Additional ratios and a sample of the above ratios calculated for a fictitious company can be found on page 67.

A final measure of a company's solvency might be calculated using the Z-score. This mathematical equation was created by Edward Altman in the early 1960s. By entering in the required values, the calculator will produce the probability of the business failing.

SUMMARY

Interpreting and understanding the financial situation of a small business does not need to be a cumbersome exercise. By paying attention to the financial health of the business, survival, success, and growth can be attained and sustained. Remember that Financial Statements are a must and include the Balance Sheet, Income Statement, and Cash Flow Statement. Budgets can be exciting and help the business run smoother. The Cash Flow Plan anticipates the future and guards against the unexpected. Finally, the process of financial management through the use of a variety of ratios will help the small business owner identify their financial health and lead them in making sound business decisions.

Glossary[9]

Amortization	The systematic allocation of the discount, premium, or issue costs of a bond to expense over the life of the bond; the systematic allocation of an intangible asset to expense over a certain period of time; the systematic reduction of a loan's principal balance through equal payment amounts which cover interest & principal repayment.
Assets	Things that are resources owned by a company and which have future economic value that can be measured and can be expressed in dollars. Examples include cash, investments, accounts receivable, inventory, supplies, land, buildings, equipment, and vehicles.
	Assets are reported on the balance sheet usually at cost or lower. Assets are also part of the accounting equation: Assets = Liabilities + Owner's (Stockholders') Equity
	Some valuable items that cannot be measured and expressed in dollars include the company's outstanding reputation, its customer base, the value of successful consumer brands, and its management team. As a result these items are not reported among the assets appearing on the balance sheet.
Audit	An examination of a company's financial statements by an independent accountant. The result is a signed opinion of whether the statements fairly reflect the company's financial results and position.
Balance Sheet	One of the main financial statements. The balance sheet reports the assets, liabilities, and owner's (stockholders') equity at a specific point in time, such as December 31. The balance sheet is also referred to as the Statement of Financial Position.
Budget	A planned level of expenditures, usually at a fairly detailed level. A company may plan and maintain a budget on either an accrual or a cash basis.
Cash Flow Management	The process of monitoring, analyzing, and adjusting your business' cash flows.
Cash Flow Statement	One of the main financial statements (along with the income statement and balance sheet). The statement of cash flows reports the sources and uses of cash by operating activities, investing activities, financing activities, and certain supplemental information for the period specified in the heading of the statement.
Current Assets	Cash and other resources that are expected to turn to cash or to be used up within one year of the balance sheet date. (If a company's operating cycle is longer than one year, an item is a current asset if it will turn to cash or be used up within the operating cycle.) Current assets are presented in the order of liquidity, i.e., cash, temporary investments, accounts receivable, inventory, supplies, prepaid insurance.

---

[9]Comprised from:

Low, Robert (2004), Accounting and Finance for Small Business Made Easy. Madison, Wisconsin:CWL Publishing Enterprises, Inc.; AccountingCoach.com (2009). Accounting Terms. Retrieved 3/5/2009 from: http://www.accountingcoach.com/accounting-terms/accounting-dictionary/index.html; and EnviroTech Financial, Inc. (2009) Financial Terms. Retrieved 3/5/2009 from: http://www.etfinancial.com/financialterms.htm

Current Liabilities	Obligations due within one year of the balance sheet date. (If a company's operating cycle is longer than one year, an item is a current liability if it is due within the operating cycle.) Another condition is that the item will use cash or it will create another current liability. (This means that if a bond payable is due within one year of the balance sheet date, but the bond will be retired by a bond sinking fund (a long term restricted asset) the bond will not be reported as a current liability.)
Depreciation	The systematic allocation of the cost of an asset from the balance sheet to Depreciation Expense on the income statement over the useful life of the asset. (The depreciation journal entry includes a debit to Depreciation Expense and a credit to Accumulated Depreciation, a contra asset account). The purpose is to allocate the cost to expense in order to comply with the matching principle. It is not intended to be a valuation process. In other words, the amount allocated to expense is not indicative of the economic value being consumed. Similarly, the amount not yet allocated is not an indication of its current market value.
Expenses	Costs that are matched with revenues on the income statement. For example, Cost of Goods Sold is an expense caused by Sales. Insurance Expense, Wages Expense, Advertising Expense, Interest Expense are expenses matched with the period of time in the heading of the income statement. Under the accrual basis of accounting, the matching is NOT based on the date that the expenses are paid.
	Expenses associated with the main activity of the business are referred to as operating expenses. Expenses associated with a peripheral activity are nonoperating or other expenses. For example, a retailer's interest expense is a nonoperating expense. A bank's interest expense is an operating expense.
	Generally, expenses are debited to a specific expense account and the normal balance of an expense account is a debit balance. When an expense account is debited, the account credited might be Cash, Accounts Payable, or Prepaid Expense depending on whether cash was paid at the time of the expense, the payment will be made after the expense was incurred, or the expense was paid in advance.
Fixed Assets	A term used when referring to property, plant, and equipment. Fixed assets other than land are depreciated.
Income Statement	One of the main financial statements (along with the balance sheet, the statement of cash flows, and the statement of stockholders' equity). The income statement is also referred to as the profit and loss statement, P&L, statement of income, and the statement of operations. The income statement reports the revenues, gains, expenses, losses, net income and other totals for the period of time shown in the heading of the statement. If a company's stock is publicly traded, earnings per share must appear on the face of the income statement.
Liabilities	Obligations of a company or organization. Amounts owed to lenders and suppliers. Liabilities often have the word "payable" in the account title. Liabilities also include amounts received in advance for a future sale or for a future service to be performed.
Loss	The result of the sale of an asset for less than its carrying amount; the write-down of assets; the net result of expenses exceeding revenues.
Owner's Equity	The book value of a company equal to the recorded amounts of assets minus the recorded amounts of liabilities.

Profit	Total revenues minus total expenses, including taxes and depreciation, for a specified time.
Revenues	Fees earned from providing services and the amounts of merchandise sold. Under the accrual basis of accounting, revenues are recorded at the time of delivering the service or the merchandise, even if cash is not received at the time of delivery. Often the term *income* is used instead of revenues. Examples of revenue accounts include: Sales, Service Revenues, Fees Earned, Interest Revenue, Interest Income. Revenue accounts are *credited* when services are performed / billed and therefore will usually have credit balances. At the time that a revenue account is credited, the account debited might be Cash, Accounts Receivable, or Unearned Revenue depending if cash was received at the time of the service, if the customer was billed at the time of the service and will pay later, or if the customer had paid in advance of the service being performed. If the revenues earned are a main activity of the business, they are considered to be operating revenues. If the revenues come from a secondary activity, they are considered to be non-operating revenues. For example, interest earned by a manufacturer on its investments is a non-operating revenue. Interest earned by a bank is considered to be part of operating revenues.
Variance	A term used with standard costs to report a difference between actual costs and standard costs.

Sample of Financial Ratios as Compared to Industry Average for a Fictitious Company[10]

Ratio	Formula	Calculation	Ratio	Industry Average	Comment
Liquidity					
Current	$\dfrac{\text{Current assets}}{\text{Current liabilities}}$	$\dfrac{\$1,000}{\$310}$	=3.2×	4.2×	Poor
Quick	$\dfrac{\text{Current assets} - \text{Inventories}}{\text{Current liabilities}}$	$\dfrac{\$385}{\$310}$	=1.2×	2.2×	Poor
Asset Management					
Inventory turnover	$\dfrac{\text{Sales}}{\text{Inventories}}$	$\dfrac{\$3,000}{\$615}$	=4.9×	10.9×	Poor
Days sales outstanding (DSO)	$\dfrac{\text{Receivables}}{\text{Annual sales}/365}$	$\dfrac{\$375}{\$8.2192}$	=46 days	36 days	Poor
Fixed assets turnover	$\dfrac{\text{Sales}}{\text{Net fixed assets}}$	$\dfrac{\$3,000}{\$1,000}$	=3.0×	2.8×	OK
Total assets turnover	$\dfrac{\text{Sales}}{\text{Total assets}}$	$\dfrac{\$3,000}{\$2,000}$	=1.5×	1.8×	Somewhat low
Debt Management					
Total debt to total assets	$\dfrac{\text{Total debt}}{\text{Total assets}}$	$\dfrac{\$1,060}{\$2,000}$	=53.0%	40.0%	High (risky)
Times-interest-earned (TIE)	$\dfrac{\text{Earnings before interest and taxes (EBIT)}}{\text{Interest charges}}$	$\dfrac{\$283.8}{\$88}$	=3.2×	6.0×	Low (risky)
EBITDA coverage	$\dfrac{\text{EBITDA} + \text{Lease payments}}{\text{Interest} + \text{Principal payments} + \text{Lease payments}}$	$\dfrac{\$411.8}{\$136}$	=3.0×	4.3×	Low (risky)
Profitability					
Profit margin on sales	$\dfrac{\text{Net income}}{\text{Sales}}$	$\dfrac{\$117.5}{\$3,000}$	=3.9%	5.0%	Poor
Return on total assets (ROA)	$\dfrac{\text{Net income}}{\text{Total assets}}$	$\dfrac{\$117.5}{\$2,000}$	=5.9%	9.0%	Poor
Basic earning power (BEP)	$\dfrac{\text{Earnings before interest and taxes (EBIT)}}{\text{Total assets}}$	$\dfrac{\$283.8}{\$2,000}$	=14.2%	18.0%	Poor
Return on common equity (ROE)	$\dfrac{\text{Net income}}{\text{Common equity}}$	$\dfrac{\$117.5}{\$940}$	=12.5%	15.0%	Poor
Market Value					
Price/earnings (P/E)	$\dfrac{\text{Price per share}}{\text{Earnings per share}}$	$\dfrac{\$23.00}{\$2.35}$	=9.8×	11.3×	Low
Price/cash flow	$\dfrac{\text{Price per share}}{\text{Cash flow per share}}$	$\dfrac{\$23.00}{\$4.35}$	=5.3×	5.4×	Low
Market/book (M/B)	$\dfrac{\text{Market price per share}}{\text{Book value per share}}$	$\dfrac{\$23.00}{\$18.80}$	=1.2×	1.7×	Low

---

[10]Brigham, E. F., Houston, J. F. (2007), Fundamentals of Financial Management, Eleventh Edition. Mason, OH: Thompson South-Western. P.119.

Measuring the 'Fiscal-Fitness' of a company: The Altman Z-Score

In the early 60's Edward Altman, using Multiple Discriminant Analysis combined a set of 5 financial ratios to come up with the Altman Z-Score. This score uses statistical techniques to predict a company's probability of failure using the following 8 variables from a company's financial statements:
The ones in Green are from the Income Statement and the ones in Red from the Balance Sheet

Use the following **Z-Score Insolvency Prediction Calculator** to assess a company.

1. Earnings Before Interest & Taxes:EBIT	1.	1600
2. Total Assets	2.	23350
3. Net Sales	3.	4000
4. Market Value of Equity	4.	3900
5. Total Liabilities	5.	15000
6. Current Assets	6.	9500
7. Current Liabilities	7.	9600 [Reset]
8. Retained Earnings	8.	2350 [Submit]

[Input your figures.The above is a sample.]

The 5 financial ratios in the Altman Z-Score and their respective weight factor is as follows:

	RATIO	WEIGHTAGE	
A	EBIT / Total Assets	x. 3.3	-4 to +8.0
B	Net Sales / Total Assets	x 0.999	-4 to +8.0
C	Market Value of Equity / Total Liabilities	x 0.6	-4 to +8.0
D	Working Capital / Total Assets	x 1.2	-4 to +8.0
E	Retained Earnings / Total Assets	x1.4	-4 to +8.0

These ratios are multiplied by the weightage as above, and the results are added together.
Z-Score = A x 3.3 + **B** x 0.99 + **C** x 0.6 + **D** x 1.2 + **E** x 1.4

The Interpretation of Z Score:

Z-SCORE ABOVE 3.0 -The company is safe based on these financial figures only.
Z-SCORE BETWEEN 2.7 and 2.99 - On Alert. This zone is an area where one should exercise caution.
Z-SCORE BETWEEN 1.8 and 2.7 - Good chances of the company going bankrupt within 2 years of operations from the date of financial figures given.
Z-SCORE BELOW 1.80- Probability of Financial embarrassment is very high.

Follow this link to access the Altman Z Score Calculator

: http://www.creditguru.com/CalcAltZ.shtml

Personal Cash Flow Plan[11]

Monthly Cash Flow Projection Made	January-09 Month 1	February-09 Month 2	March-09 Month 3	April-09 Month 4	May-09 Month 5	June-09 Month 6	July-09 Month 7	August-09 Month 8	September-09 Month 9	October-09 Month 10	November-09 Month 11	December-09 Month 12	Year Total
BEGINNING CASH		0	0	0	0	0	0	0	0	0	0	0	0
Deposit Account Balance													0
Other Cash Balances													0
Monthly Income													
Salary/Wages - Self													0
Salary/Wages - Spouse													0
Child Support / Alimony													0
Social Security/Unemployment													0
Other Income													0
TOTAL CASH AVAILABLE	0	0	0	0	0	0	0	0	0	0	0	0	0
EXPENSES													
Mortgage/Rent													
Property Taxes													
Property Insurance													
Home Equity Line of Credit													
Gas Bill													
Electricity													
Water Bill													
Telephone													
Credit Cards													
Auto Loan													
Auto Insurance													
Day Care Expense													
Fuel Expense													
Food													
Clothing													
Recreational													
Other													
Sub Total of Expenses	0	0	0	0	0	0	0	0	0	0	0	0	0
Contingency (10% of Expenses)	0	0	0	0	0	0	0	0	0	0	0	0	0
TOTAL EXPENSES	0	0	0	0	0	0	0	0	0	0	0	0	0
ENDING CASH TOTALS	0	0	0	0	0	0	0	0	0	0	0	0	0

---

[11] Women's Business Development Center (2009). Retrieved on 3/4/2009 from: http://www.wbdc.org/AlreadyInBusiness/Financing.aspx

Internal Control Questionnaire for Cash Disbursements[12]

Internal Controls can provide protection from loss and errors. Use this Questionnaire to determine if you have established effective internal controls in the area of cash disbursements.

Accessibility or Safeguarding

Physical controls and restricted access are important control tools. Review this section to see if your procedures can use improvement.

Yes	No	
		Are all payments made by check or other negotiable instruments?
		Are checks made payable to specific payees?
		Are your checks pre-numbered and used in sequence?
		Are voided, special or mutilated checks saved and filed?
		Does someone check the sequence of checks periodically?
		Do you store unused checks in a restricted area in the possession of a specified person?
		Are checks made of protective paper?
		Is a check protector used?
		If you use facsimile plates or similar devices for check signatures, have you identified who is to have custody and use of the plates?
		Do you keep facsimile plates in a restricted, secure place apart from blank check stock? Are the plates used only in the presence of the person designated as responsible?

---

[12]Low, Robert (2004), Accounting and Finance for Small Business Made Easy. Madison, Wisconsin: CWL Publishing Enterprises, Inc. pp. 286-289.

Separation of Duties

Maintaining a distinct Separation of Duties is one of the most important practices you can establish for controlling unauthorized expenditures, theft, and errors.

Yes	No	
		Are checks prepared by persons other than those with voucher approval authority?
		Is the person who prepares checks independent of purchasing and receiving functions?
		Are checks signed by persons other than those preparing or having approval authority?
		Are authorized signatures limited to employees having no access to accounting records, cash receipts, or petty cash funds?
		Is there a dollar limit at which all checks must be countersigned?
		Are bank reconciliations prepared monthly by an employee who does not sign checks, records cash transactions or have access to cash?
		Does this person receive the bank statement unopened?

Processing and Recording

Review the questions below to check whether your Processing and Recording procedures provide enough checks and balances to detect incorrect transactions.

Yes	No	
		Are all regular disbursements that you make by checks prepared and based on adequate and approved documentation?
		Does the person who signs checks verify whether the amounts are approved and have adequate documentation?
		Do you pay only against original invoices and not against statements or photocopies?
		Do you mark invoices after payment and check for duplicate numbers to avoid paying twice?
		Are only complete checks – not blank – ever signed?
		After signing, are all checks recorded in a cash disbursement record that gives enough detail to allow accurate summarizing and posting?
		Are actual disbursements periodically compared with forecasted disbursements and larger or unusual variances investigated and accounted for?

Case Study – Stabilizing a Business

How would they stabilize their business? What strategy would you put in place? Identify the Key Indicators that their business is stabilized.

What can they do to continue to stabilize their business?

Key Point: Never stop paying attention to what matters most: Cash Flow.

Transform ~ Stabilize ~ **Grow** ~ Innovate

Marketing Strategies

Growing a business is not as easy as paying for advertising and waiting for your customers to open your door. It takes careful identification of WHO your customers are and HOW you are going to reach them.

That's not new, but what are the tools that we use to reach our customers who may be on the other side of the globe? You need to literally reach out and touch someone you can't see or understand when they speak.

How Do You Grow a Business?

There are three basic ways to grow your business:
1. Increase the number of customers
2. Increase the number of times each customer buys
3. Increase the quantity that is sold each time

You can increase the number of customers using your existing product or service or you can increase the offering. You can expand your existing market or reach into new markets, but do your homework first. Which markets will be the most profitable?

Make it easy for your existing customers to do business with you. Be responsive to your customer's calls; be accessible when they contact you; be consistent with your offering; follow-up and follow through; and be accurate and timely with your billing.

Determine how you can add value and expand your service offering. Stay customer focused and you will build a foundation for generating more sales, retaining more customers, and growing your business.

List ways to grow your business. Be creative and think outside the box.

1.
2.
3.
4.
5.
6.
7.
8.

Case Study – Growing a Business

How can they grow their business? Identify WHO their customers are and HOW they are going to reach them to grow the business.

How can they continue to grow their business?

Key Point: Never Stop Growing the Business!

Developing a Seven-Touch Marketing Plan (7-TMP™)

A Marketing Plan is vital to the survival and success of a small business. When resources are limited, it becomes even more important that the plan identify how to reach the customers who will buy the specific product or service. When competing for customers, the business that makes the fewest mistakes will be the survivor. Planning to fail is the result of marketing without a plan.

It takes more than one time to reach a customer. Research indicates that it requires seven touches with a consistent message to make a sale.

Step One: Know who your customers are.

Who do you sell to? Who do you want to sell to? Are your customers consumers, other businesses, or government agencies? Each customer is a separate Target Market. Describe one of your customers in as much detail as you can.

Where does your customer go to get information about your product or service?

1.	
2.	
3.	
4.	
5.	
6.	
7.	
8.	

Step Two: Know the benefits of your product or service from your customer's perspective.

Look at your product or service and define the benefits to the customers. Features are nice, but they don't make the sale. Your customer must be convinced that the benefit is worth the cost to purchase the product or service. The benefit for each customer will be different. If you sell to both consumers and other businesses, create two lists of benefits AND create two separate Marketing Plans.

Product / Service	Customer	Benefit

From your list of benefits, create a message that will resonate with each of your customers. It is important that the message is consistent.

Step Three: Connect your customer with the message.

This step is all about the tools. At Party Pro they used the Internet and a robust Web site to reach their customers. How do you reach your customers?

1.	
2.	
3.	
4.	
5.	
6.	
7.	
8.	

Putting an ad in a newspaper ONCE is not an example of an effective Marketing Strategy. Review the material in the Appendix to identify new methods that you can use to reach your customers seven times.

Select one method to reach your customers. How much will it cost to implement that marketing method? How many times will you need to utilize the method to consistently reach your customer base? What are the risks? When do you expect results? Is your plan S.M.A.R.T.?

Describe one method you can use to touch your customer. How is this different from plans to reach other Target Markets? How will you separate the messages to ensure that the customers only hear the message that is targeting them?

Web Site – A Tool

A Web site is a tool to reach more customers but like any tool, (i.e., hammer, shovel, rolling pin, etc.) the tool will not be used without a human hand to guide it. You have to direct the use of your Web site. You need to advertise using other methods to drive customers to the Web site. A Web site is the perfect place to state the message. Elaborate on the benefits to the customers. It is easy to create multiple messages for multiple customers (Target Markets).

How can you use a Web site to grow your business? What methods are can you use to ensure your customers read your message?

1.	
2.	
3.	
4.	
5.	
6.	
7.	
8.	

What are your S.M.A.R.T. Goals for your Web site?

Seven-Touch Marketing Plan (7-TMP™)

1. Determine your Target Market(s).

2. Select seven methods to touch your current and potential customers.

3. Decide on the frequency that you are going to use the method.

4. Calculate the cost for each method and total cost.

5. Adjust the method and frequency until the total cost is less than what you have in your budget.

	Target Market	Seven Touch Methods	Frequency	Cost
1				
2				
3				
4				
5				
6				
7				
Total Cost				

Major Media Types

Media	Advantages	Limitations	Cost*
Newspapers	Flexibility; timeliness; good local market coverage; broad acceptability; high believability	Short life; poor reproduction quality; small pass-along audience	$1,300 / week for 2" x 2" ad This depends on the newspaper!
Television	Good mass market coverage; low cost per exposure; combines sight, sound, and motion; appealing to the senses	High absolute costs; high clutter; fleeting exposure; less audience selectivity	$200,000 for one 30-second commercial (during prime-time)
Direct mail	High audience selectivity; flexibility; no ad competition within the same medium; allows personalization	Relatively high cost per exposure; "junk mail" image	$1,500 for 1,000 4x6 postcards (includes postage)
Radio	Good local acceptance; high geographic and demographic selectivity; low cost	Audio only, fleeting exposure; low attention (the half-heard" medium); fragmented audiences	$90 to $120 per week on a rotator (prices higher if time slots for ad are selective)
Magazines	High and demographic selectivity; credibility and prestige; high-quality reproduction; long life and good pass-along readership	Long ad purchase lead time; high cost; no guarantee of position	$1,200 to $5,000 per month or per issue (depends on ad size and demo-graphics)
Outdoor (Bill Board)	Flexibility; high repeat exposure; low cost; low message competition; good positional selectivity	Little audience selectivity, creative limitations	$3,000 artwork; $5,000 to $500,000; mini-mum contract is 16 weeks
Online	High selectivity; low cost; immediacy; interactive capabilities	Small, demographical-ly skewed audience; relatively low impact; audience controls exposure	$0.60 pay-per-click, $1,800/ month aggressive cam-paigns; $200 to $1,200 per year per banner ad

*prices include price break for a 12 week campaign.

www.iesmallbusiness.com/resources

10 Ways to Grow Your Business

In an article written in May 2004, Karen E. Spaeder correctly assesses the situation that many of you are in today. You spent considerable time and energy to get your business off the ground and now you are in a quandary on how to take your business to the next level.

"For those of you who have survived startup and built successful businesses, you may be wondering how to take the next step and grow your business beyond its current status." Choosing the proper strategy now will make the difference between success and failure. What growth strategy you define in your Strategic Plan "will depend on the type of business you own, your available resources, and how much money, time, and sweat equity you're willing to invest all over again."

1. **Open another location.** Before you take the leap and open another location, consider the research that was required before you opened the current locations. Choosing a new location requires careful research, planning and number-crunching.

   - Make sure you create a business plan for each new location.
   - Make sure you KNOW your management team and are prepared with a Plan B.
   - Watch the bottom line!!
   - Always choose a location that is best for the business not what is best for your wallet.

2. **Offer your business as a franchise or business opportunity.** Franchising is a model for expansion with an operating system that allows ownership on the part of the staff operating the franchise. The franchisee has a vested interest in the success of the business. Begin by networking within the franchise community and become a member of the International Franchise Association. Find a good franchise attorney as well as a mentor who's been through the franchise process.

3. **License your product.** Licensing minimizes your risk and is low cost in comparison to the price of starting your own company to produce and sell your brand or product. Before you license your product, make sure you work with an intellectual property attorney to ensure you don't lose control of your product or service.

4. **Form an alliance.** Select alliances and companies that mutually benefit from the relationship. Similar to the hot dog and hot dog bun, some businesses dovetail and enable you to expand your business without increasing your risk. Some are as simple as adding a link to your Web site and receiving a commission on the number of clicks. The key is to make sure the alliances are relevant. You need to align yourself with businesses that already have clients.

5. **Diversify.** Diversifying is an excellent growth strategy because it allows you to have multiple streams of income that can often fill seasonal voids, such as snow plowing in the winter and landscaping in the summer. Speaking and writing complement each other and can increase sales and profit margins. Often Business Plans include ideas on diversification. New services, new products, and new target markets are forms of diversification.

6. **Target other markets.** Expand into uncharted territory and open new markets. Go global and retrofit your product so you can approach a new market. Brainstorm ideas on how your product or service can be used by a new group of customers.

7. **Win a government contract.** The U.S. government is the largest buyer of goods and services in the world, with total procurement dollars reaching approximately $235 billion in 2002. Work with the ISBDC or PTAC (http://wpdi.clcillinois.edu/ptac/). Patience is a requirement when working with the government. Requests for proposals usually require a significant amount of groundwork and research. If you're not prepared to take the time to fully comply with RFP terms and conditions, you'll only be wasting your time. The end result is worth it if you win a bid, because you generally do not have to go to the same legwork next time.

8. **Merge with or acquire another business.** While on the surface this can appear to be a great opportunity and it can be very successful, there are a number of issues that must be addressed: Customer retention, staff retention, technologies integration, and defining the culture.

9. **Expand globally.** You can go global with any of the solutions already mentioned, but you just need to build an international strategy that considers the need for a foreign distributor who will carry an inventory of your product and resell it in their domestic markets. You can locate foreign distributors by scouring your city or state for a foreign company with a U.S. representative. Trade groups, foreign chambers of commerce in the United States, and branches of American chambers of commerce in foreign countries are also good places to find distributors you can work with.

10. **Expand to the Internet.** "Bill Gates said that by the end of 2002, there will be only two kinds of businesses: Those with an Internet presence, and those with no business at all," notes Sally Falkowa, Pasadena, California, Web content strategist. "Perhaps this is overstating the case, but an effective Web site is becoming an integral part of business today." The focus is on Search Engine Optimization and keeping your customer on your site so they will buy your product or service.

You need a Web site that is ranked high enough to ensure adequate traffic and a designed well enough that it looks professional, but most important is to have content that is relevant so it draws in visitors and they stay.

Marketing Misconceptions

Written by Andrew Bordeaux on Wednesday, July 23, 2008

For the growing business, the implementation of carefully targeted, high-quality marketing initiatives can make all the difference. The world of marketing, however, consists of a broad amalgamation of techniques and sub-disciplines that should, ideally, work harmoniously to convey what people need to know about your business. How does a company ensure that they've maximized the variety of options that marketing can provide?

Guerilla Marketing guru Jay Conrad Levinson recently wrote his thoughts on the most frequent mistakes companies make with their marketing initiatives. Through a list of 11 missteps, the problems are effectively boiled down to three main misconceptions:

1) The heart of marketing lies in the superficial, the "whiz-bang," or the punch-line.
2) A business only needs one marketing mechanism at a time.
3) If the marketing is good enough, the results will be quick and earth-shattering.

The first of these errors takes hold when marketing executives lose site of their main purpose, which is to motivate people. Distracted from the primary mission, they might aim for a clever or humorous marketing stratagem. This is a trap. While humor or cleverness can successfully engage a potential client or customer, chances are those elements will overshadow the product or service you've set out to promote. Similarly, too much emphasis on entertaining your audience can eclipse your product or service as well. The job at hand is to make the truth fascinating – not to entertain for the sake of entertaining.

The second common mistake, especially in the case of many small businesses, is under-executing-- implementing only a pinch of the marketing ingredients at your disposal. Marketing areas such as direct mail, telemarketing, brochures, or phone-book advertisements, when executed properly, can provide a fantastic ROI for the growing company. Any of these elements alone, however, is just a drop in the bucket and can prevent you from reaching the full breadth of your target audience. Diversifying your marketing initiatives isn't an extravagance – it's a necessity.

The last, and arguably the biggest, misconception is that marketing is a "panacea" for the business; one that results in customers breaking down your doors moments after the launch of a campaign. It is true that strong marketing efforts will (and should!) correlate to increased profits, but it's seldom overnight, and it's wrong to expect miracles. As will many other aspects of growing a business, patience is a virtue.

So if these are the misconceptions, what is a true picture of marketing? As stated by Levinson, "Marketing is an opportunity for you to earn profits with your business, a chance to cooperate with other businesses in your community or your industry and a process of building lasting relationships."

Transform ~ Stabilize ~ Grow ~ **Innovate**

Innovation Strategies

Innovation is perhaps one of the most critical skills required of the small business owner as the leader of their company. Many times when we think of the term "innovation" the image of a great inventor or politician or renowned giant of business comes to mind. Sometimes it conjures up the notion of "thinking outside the box." The fact is that the term innovation is really a process and like any process, it must be managed very well to be successful. There are three primary components that a small business owner must provide if they are to implement innovation within their company. These components are also the make-up of entrepreneurial leaders. The three components are: 1) Leadership; 2) Access to Funding; and 3) Accountability.

Leadership

A brief review of history teaches us that innovation and transformation occur during times of economic turmoil. Entrepreneurial leaders are the first to spot this phenomenon and seize the opportunities, complete with all the risks that go along with taking that action. They realize that in order to move their business forward, they can no longer carry the weight of the business alone. They look out among those they know and begin to delegate authority, empower their workforces, and hire individuals to manage the coming change.

Notice that the entrepreneurial leader needs individuals that can organize and manage the work. As entrepreneurs, they already recognize and understand that they do not need people like themselves who are catalysts in making change happen. They require administrators and supervisors and other types of management with leadership skills. But do not underestimate the primary need to delegate and empower these individuals.

It is one thing to delegate or empower and another to communicate clearly the responsibilities of these individuals. In other words, lip service is unacceptable. The management team must know what is expected, when, and by what measures they will be held accountable. The management team may be less holistic in understanding the big picture and more tactical in their organizing of activities, so the entrepreneurial leader must continue to lead innovation from the perspective of the entire organization. If the leader cannot do this, they must accept the fact that it may be time to step aside for the good of the whole.

The coming change is the beginning of innovations. When asked to define the term innovation, management consultant and CEO of PROCESOi, Mariana Ferrari Quijano, stated in her article on innovation, "…it is better not to define it, but to accept all its synonyms: change, alteration, revolution, upheaval, transformation, metamorphosis, breakthrough; new measures, new methods, modernization, novelty, newness; creativity, originality, ingenuity, inspiration, inventiveness, shake up."[13]

---

[13] Quijano, M. F. (2009). "Innovation: What's in that little trendy sexy word?". Techman / Kanata. Retrieved on 3/15/09 from: http://www.techmankanata.com/ar-104-pg-1/Innovation-whats-in-that-little-trendy.htm

However, when asked to define an innovator, her response was, "An innovator is defined, as an individual, who has a global way of thinking, is intuitive, takes risks, is imaginative, and often breaks the rules."[14] She sums up her article with these lasting words: "Innovation is a synonym for Joy and Happiness, and should not be made a "serious business strategy." Joy, because creating, learning, making mistakes is fun, and happiness because achieving far-fetched, almost unbelievable results makes everybody happy. Don't just take my word, ask Steve Jobs."[15]

Access to Funding

Innovation is not funded by the hope and aspiration of dreams. It requires a dedicated financial commitment. This does not mean that the entrepreneurial leader must break the bank. What it means is that those who have been given delegation authority, empowerment and / or management responsibility clearly understand that an environment has been established which will financially foster innovation.

So the goal is to create an environment where innovation can be nurtured and grown through studying, learning, teaching, failing, and succeeding. Mariana calls it an innovation factory where employees are challenged to examine the current business environment by:

1. looking ahead,

2. projecting the future,

3. identifying future needs and

4. creating solutions for those needs

She calls this Innovation Capacity - by encouraging employees to be more creative and providing them opportunities to experiment, rewarding innovative work behaviors that result in successes, and implementing real innovation practices that allows you to build an innovation factory.

---

[14] Ibid.

[15] Dalal, Sanjay. (3/7/09). "Creativity and Innovation".   Retrieved on 3/14/09 from: http://creativityandinnovation.blogspot.com/

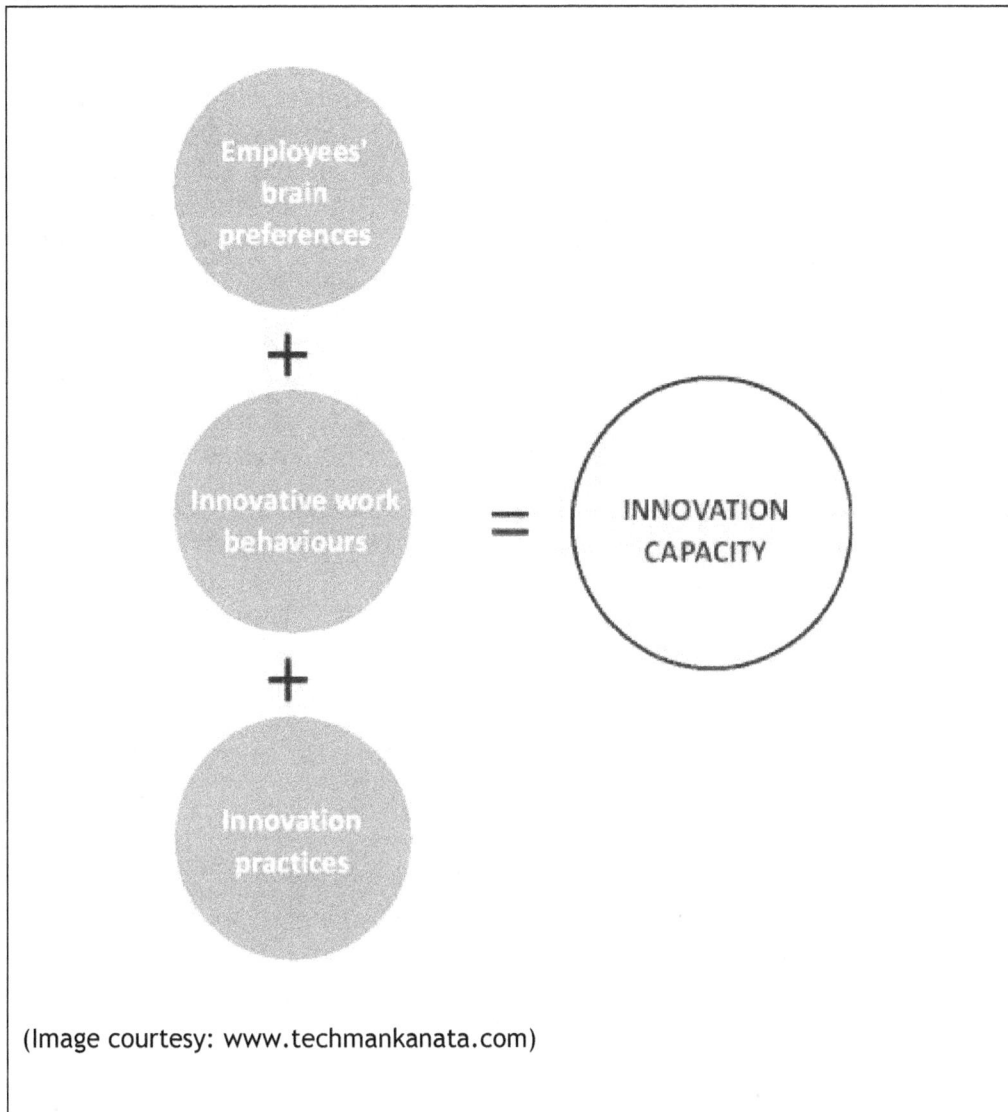

(Image courtesy: www.techmankanata.com)

What is the payoff of creating an environment modeled like the above? Probably the most significant benefit is a higher probability of creating a competitive advantage. Anytime a business is able to stay focused on the future, (i.e., forward looking) and can deliver solutions for the issues that will arise, it will leave the competition behind. Mariana uses Procesoi as an example stating, "At PROCESOi we consider innovation to be a strategy, to increase a company's present value, keep it ahead of its competitors and create sustainable growth."

So, if the benefit of innovation can be a competitive advantage with sustainable growth, what is the cost? Going back to what was said earlier, we can now see that the cost is not necessarily in hard dollars for capital expense, but rather an investment in the people of the organization. The costs will be focused on addressing the needs of the employees, preparing them for innovation and change, and tracking the progress as the organization moves forward. Access to funding means implementing and innovation-friendly environment and providing a financial budget in which it can thrive.

Accountability

As the entrepreneurial leader prepares the organization for innovation and change, the third component is not lost on their instinct for success. Success is a measure and to ensure success, measurements must be put in place to gage the forward progression of the changes the organization is facing. Accountability refers to all the necessary measurements. Employees must be held accountable and before they can be, job descriptions, expectations, and incentives must be documented. Communications must be clear, precise, and understandable as well as continuous. A safe learning environment where failures are considered necessary steps toward success must be established (Innovation Factory). Regular reviews to monitor progress and assess direction are required. In the simplest terms of project management, the process steps are: Plan, Implement, Review, and Revise.

A major part of the accountability element is in managing the change. This is actually a continuous and ongoing process to make sure all strategies, objectives, goals and tactics are aligned. It is very strategic in nature. According to the Graziadio Business Report from Pepperdine University, there are six principles to managing change in the business environment.

These six principles are:[16]

1. "Do no harm. The best defense against doing no harm is to take a holistic approach.

2. All change involves personal choice. Change is more often resisted than supported in organizations because people rarely are given the chance to understand the reason for the change.

3. The relationship between change and performance is not instantaneous. Change involves time and the opportunity to learn, and learning is often inefficient. So don't expect performance improvement too quickly.

4. Connect change to business strategy. Change should only be pursued in the context of a clear goal, be it personal, group, organizational, or societal.

5. Involvement breeds commitment. The lesson is that involving people in change decisions provides improved estimates of time tables, expectations, and commitment.

6. Any good change effort results in increased capacity to face change in the future."[17]

---

[16] Worley, C. G. , Vick, Y. H. (2009). "Leading and Managing Change". Retrieved on 2/15/09 from http://gbr.pepperdine.edu/052/change.html

[17] Ibid.

Sustainability

Once the innovation process has been established, the entrepreneurial small business owner recognizes that it is indeed a process and not a project which comes to an end. On the contrary, the process is a cycle of continuous improvement or more pointedly, sustainable success. It is the basic foundation of the competitive advantage in that it responds to the rapid changes of the business environment. When viewed from the perspective of the total organization, it is the most important value-creating asset of the business.

As was mentioned above, reviews are conducted in the accountability element of the innovation process. This is a good time to consider growth strategies and making sure the business is working effectively and efficiently. Effective work is considered to be the "things" the business is doing correctly. Efficient work is "how well" the business performs. The small business owner will keep the organization focused on innovation by examining what and how the business is working.

Additionally, they might consider some of the following:

- How do we decide which markets to focus on?
- Who are our best customers?
- Who are our real competitors?
- What sets us apart?
- How do we turn a brand into a compelling proposition to the marketplace?
- How do we make networks work best for us?

During this cycle of continuous improvement, the innovative entrepreneurial small business owner will connect the unconnected, challenge the status quo, look ahead for new opportunities, and will be seen as the risk taker who is not afraid to try out a new idea. It all begins by looking ahead into the future and from outside of the box.

"The goal of innovation is positive change, to make someone or something better. Innovation leading to increased productivity is the fundamental source of increasing wealth in an economy." [18]

---

[18] Business Innovation (2009). Retrieved 3/14/09 from: http://business-innovation.com/

Case Study – Business Innovation

What is innovative about this business? Identify WHO their customers are and HOW they are going to reach them as they innovate the business.

How can they continue to be innovative in their business?

Key Point: Innovation is the strength of Small Business!

Bringing It All Together

What is important in your personal life? What is important to your business? Your life is a journey and it is important to make decisions that will lead you toward your desired destination. You set priorities that indicate what is important to you.

What are your long-term goals? Will going into business assist or prevent you from going where you want to go?

Your business goals only define one dimension of your life. The goals you set for each dimension will affect the others, so don't set goals in just one area. Consider what you want to accomplish while considering the impact on all of the areas.

	This Year	Five Years	Life
Spiritual and Emotional			
Physical and Health			
Education			
Family and Friends			
Financial			
Social and Community			
Employment			

Future Business Goals

A Strategic Plan is a collection of business goals that guide the business as it grows and expands. Priorities are set and realistic deliverables defined. Goals should be S.M.A.R.T. – Specific, Measurable, Achievable, Relevant, and Time Bound.

A Five-Year Game Plan is a simple Strategic Plan that is formatted on one page for easy reference. The first step is to clarify the Vision and the Mission for the organization. The Vision is where you want to be in five years. It is not who you are but where you want to be. The Mission is how you are going to accomplish the Vision. It is the key to successfully reaching the destination established in the Vision. Strategies are the practical directives that support the Mission.

The Plan includes a maximum of five strategies. To accomplish the strategies, no more than six objectives (strategic objectives) are defined. The objectives are specific, with measurable results produced while implementing strategies. The next step includes identifying specific tasks to implement the objectives. The tasks are assigned to an individual who is responsible to complete the task by a specified date.

One Page Game Plan

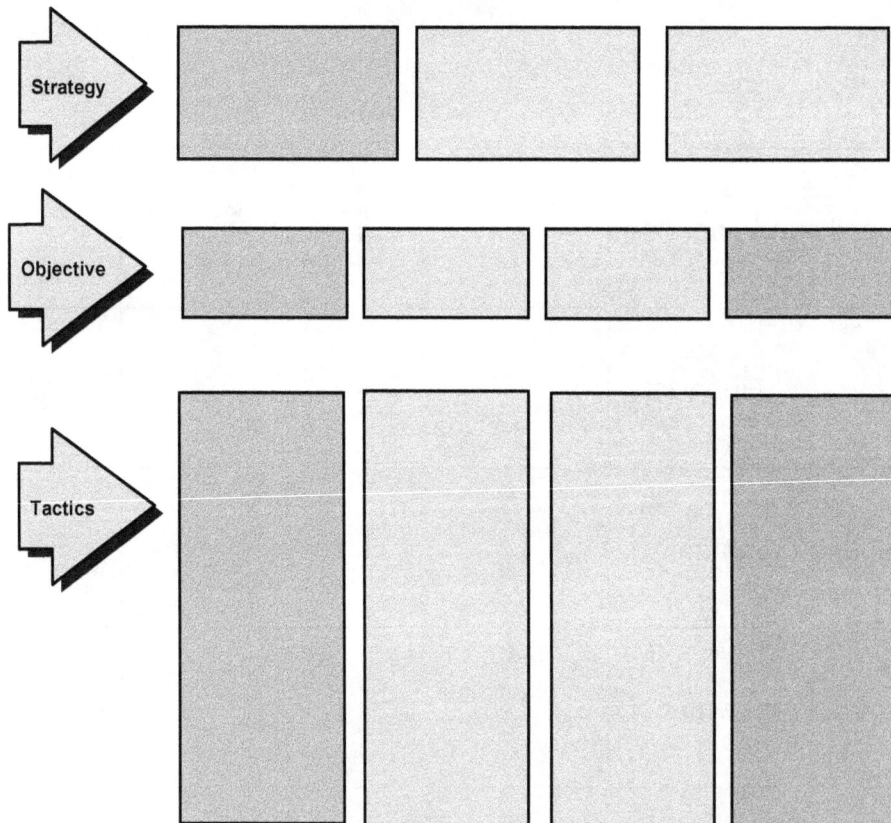

Strategic Exercise

Define the Purpose, Mission, and Vision of your organization?

What is your strategy to Transform your business?

What is your strategy to Stabilize your business?

What is your strategy to Grow your business?

What is your strategy to Innovate your business?

How will you celebrate achievements?

Making It Happen

Your 1-PSP is a living document that should change and evolve over time. Where are you on the timeline continuum? Are you still in the initial stage of exploring ideas? Do you have a Business Plan that you think will work for you? Have you developed plans to accomplish the milestones in your 1-PSP? Are you making the progress you expected? Do you want to change your direction? Identify what you have accomplished and what you need to work on. Decide what's on first and list it below. You are in the driver's seat, so make it happen.

Your Challenge

Today, find a trusted advisor who you can report where you are in the business planning process; then check in monthly, telling the advisor where you are on the journey. They are your lifeline to Business Survival!

Remember to pay attention to what matters most and transform, stabilize, grow, and innovate your business to achieve sustainable success using the simple planning cycle to **SPIR** (Strategize, Plan, Implement, and Reflect).

Work your Plan because only you can pull your Vision together!

Appendix A: Web Sites for Business

Illinois Small Business Development Center - http://wpdi.clcillinois.edu/sbdc/

Naming Your Business:

Illinois - www.cyberdriveillinois.com/departments/business_services/corp.html

Trademark / Service Mark - www.uspto.gov

      TESS - tess2.uspto.gov/bin/gate.exe?f=tess&state=5970pg.1.1

Domain Name - www.networksolutions.com

Software:

www.paloalto.com

www.intuit.com

Small Business:

www.census.gov

www.score.org

www.askjim.biz

www.smallbusinessadvocate.com

www.sba.gov

office.microsoft.com/en-us/templates/default.aspx

www.tannedfeet.com - Legal information

www.ienconnect.com – Illinois Entrepreneurial Network - State resources

www.irs.gov/businesses/small/index.html

www.bls.gov/OCO

State of Illinois

www.state.il.us/dcfs/index.shtml - Department of Children and Family Services

www.idfpr.com - Illinois Department of Professional Regulations – licensing

www.revenue.state.il.us - Illinois Department of Revenue

Through local Libraries use Reference USA (InfoUSA) to obtain a list of competitors in specific geographic areas. The data can also be used to look for sales leads, find new business opportunities, and track phone numbers and addresses for public and private companies.

Appendix B: References

"Growing Your Business Through Principled Networking" by Julia Hubbel and published by Ernst & Young LLP.

Jim Blasingame, http://www.smallbusinessadvocate.com/

Andrea Nierenberg, http://www.smallbusinessadvocate.com/small-business-braintrust/andrea-nierenberg-377

Boomer, L. Gary (06/24/05) "Tips for holding a successful accounting firm summit" Microsoft Dynamics. Retrieved 2/10/09 from: http://www.microsoft.com/dynamics/accountingprofessionals/ap_boomer_firmsummit.mspx#EPC

Mind Tools Ltd, (2009), Using the TOWS Matrix. Retrieved on 2/11/09 from: http://www.mindtools.com/pages/article/newSTR_89.htm

Orme, Denis, (2007), "Your Leading Ways Newsletter", No. 23. Retrieved 2/11/09 from: http://www.leader-success.com/newsletter23.htm

Payne, Stephen G. (10/10/06), "Driving Growth Through Leadership" Princeton Regional Chamber of Commerce, 2006 Fall Workshop Slide Presentation, Retrieved 2/17/09 from: http://www.leaderx.com/multimedia/PRCC_Growth_Workshop_PreWork.ppt#279,1 ,Slide 1

Drucker, Peter F. (1954), "The Practice of Management", New York: New York, HarperCollins Publishers, Inc., 10 East 53rd Street.

Nikitina, Arina (2008), Retrieved on 2/07/09 from: http://www.goal-setting-guide.com/smart-goals.html

Wikipedia (2008), Retrieved on 2/10/09 from: http://en.wikipedia.org/wiki/SMART_(project_management)

Wiley Publishing Co. (2009), Retrieved on 2/11/09 from: http://www.dummies.com/how-to/content/setting-smart-management-goals.html

Insights - Insights Learning & Development Ltd, Jack Martin Way, Claverhouse Business Park, Dundee DD4 9FF, Scotland, UK, T: +44 (0)1382 908050 F: +44 (0)1382 908051 E:insights@insights.com www.insights.com

Sargent, D., Sargent, M., Wold, D. P. (September, 2005). " Part VIII: Managing Your Money". NxLeveL® Guide for Entrepreneurs, Fourth Edition. USA:NxLeveL® Education Foundation.

Osmond, J. H. (2005), A Business Survival Workbook. Lake Villa, IL:The Vision Tree, Ltd.

Brigham, E. F., Houston, J. F. (2007), Fundamentals of Financial Managerment, Eleventh Edition. Mason, OH: Thompson South-Western.

Fry, F. L. Ph.D., Stoner, C. R. Ph.D., and Weinzimmer, L. G. Ph.D., (2005). "Running the Numbers", Strategic Planning for Small Business Made Easy. Madison, Wisconsin:CWL Publishing Enterprises, Inc.

Low, Robert (2004), Accounting and Finance for Small Business Made Easy. Madison, Wisconsin:CWL Publishing Enterprises, Inc.

Williams, Jan R.; Susan F. Haka, Mark S. Bettner, Joseph V. Carcello (2008). *Financial & Managerial Accounting*. McGraw-Hill Irwin.

Ward, Susan (2008). "Cash Flow Management". About.com Retrieved on 3/4/2008 from: http://sbinfocanada.about.com/cs/management/g/cashflowmgt.htm

Growing Your Business (December 11, 2003). "How To Better Manage Your Cash Flow". Entreprenuer.com. Retrieved 3/4/2008 from:

http://www.entrepreneur.com/money/moneymanagement/managingcashflow/article66008.html

Epstein, Barry J.; Eva K. Jermakowicz (2007). Interpretation and Application of International Financial Reporting Standards. John Wiley & Sons. p. 1

Karen E. Spaeder, "10 Ways to Grow You're Business", May 11, 2004, http://www.entrepreneur.com/interstitial/Ent_Interstitial.aspx?URL=/management/growingyourbusiness/article70660.html

Andrew Bordeaux, "Marketing Misconceptions", July 23, 2008, Grow Think, http://www.growthink.com/content/3-common-marketing-misconceptions

Appendix C: Forms

Seven-Touch Marketing Plan (7-TMP™)

One-Page Strategic Plan (1-PSP™)

One-Page Strategic Indicators (1-PSI™)

Seven-Touch Marketing Plan (7-TMP™)

This report indicates the customers, the methods used to penetrate the market, and the estimated budget necessary to implement the Marketing Strategy.

	Target Market	Seven-Touch Methods	Frequency	Cost
1				
2				
3				
4				
5				
6				
7				
Total Cost				

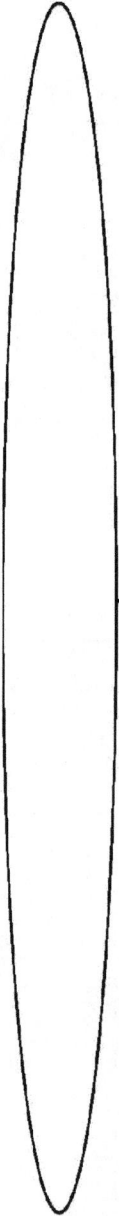
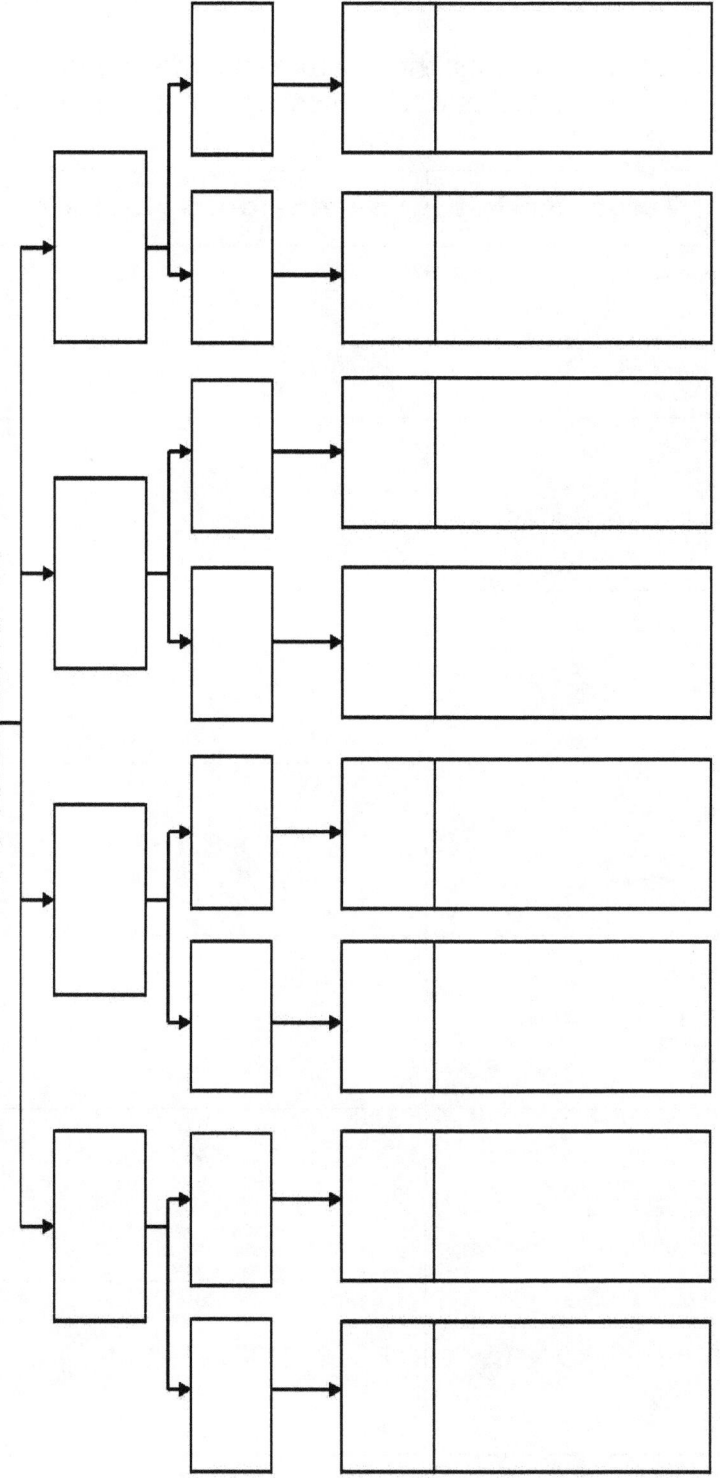

1-PSP™

1-Page Strategic Indicators™ (1-PSI™)

Strategic Area	Objective	Goal	Tactics	When/How Measured	Results	Achieved?

STATUS ● ○ ●

Joanne Osmond

Joanne Osmond is a reformer and change agent. She has been recognized over the years for transforming both individuals and organizations. While at Abbott Laboratories, Joanne received an international award, the **2000 Help Desk Institute's Team Excellence Award**. This is an award for operational excellence by developing the right organization, processes, and technology to provide consistent delivery of end-to-end customer support. In 2003, she received the **ATHENA Award** for assisting women in reaching their full leadership potential while demonstrating excellence, creativity, and initiative in her profession.

She is the recipient of the Boy Scout's coveted Silver Beaver Award and serves on the Council's Executive Board as the Vice President of Cub Scouting. She has served on the Lake Villa Elementary School Board for 16 years, elected to serve her fourteenth year on Lake's Division of the IASB, and was recently elected to the IASB's executive board. In addition, she serves on the SEDOL's Executive Board. As the owner and President of Market Drafters, she works with the Small Business Development Center in assisting entrepreneurs move to the next level. Her current focus is Web Hosting and Design for small businesses, professionals, Individuals, groups, families, and not-for-profit organizations. She partners with her clients to drive search engine optimization and self-management of the site by the owner to create sustainable success. To contact Joanne Osmond e-Mail her at Jo@TheVisionTree.com.

Claudia Pannell

Claudia Pannell is a business coach with The Vision Tree, Ltd. and counselor for the Illinois Small Business Development Center. Both positions help clients address today's business challenges. Clients seeking assistance come from small, medium and large businesses and include individual owners to Fortune 500 management teams. Prior to joining The Vision Tree, Ltd., Claudia spent 15 years at Abbott in Dallas, Texas and Lake County, Illinois. While at Abbott, she served as a Computer Analyst, Project Leader, and Systems Manager. Additionally, she served as a corporate mentor and Officer of the IT Women's Leadership Network. During her time at Abbott, she successfully honed her leadership skills and often served as a facilitator for strategic planning sessions.

Claudia offers her clients a wide range of programs and services including workshops for teambuilding, problem solving, project management, innovation, change management and strategic planning. Most activities are designed for clients to identify problem areas of their organization, analyze potential solutions and develop manageable action plans that can be implemented to improve the situation.

Claudia is no stranger to the business environment. She spent a combined 10 years as a business professional for IBM, Kaiser Aluminum and as the owner of a retail lumber specialty company in North Texas. This provided her the foundation needed when addressing the ever-changing business environment.

Her book Business Survival for Project Management is scheduled for publication in 2009 and is designed to assist individuals seeking certification in project management by the Project Management Institute. To contact Claudia Pannell, e-Mail her at Claudia@TheVisionTree.com.